The View from the Bottom 2015

By Steven L. Kyer

TABLE OF CONTENTS

PREFACE

In 1993, I pressured myself into sitting down and writing what average people tend to think about the issues confronting Americans in the modern world. Although I don't hold all the views expressed, they take from my own and include many I have heard over the years.

The important point is that I wanted to provide some balance to the pompous contrived ideas of the powerful and well placed. They seem to dominate all discussion, as if their views are more important and always more informed that those of an average American.

A very conservative friend liked the original version so much for its balance that he gave a copy to the Florida Speaker of the House and another to Jeb Bush, one time governor of that state. He suggested some time ago, that I should update it and republish as an ebook. So it was that I set out to do just that early in 2015.

A View from the Bottom is an attempt to fill a void in the information that flies at us from all sides daily. For years I have shared the frustration I think all Americans feel at the attitudes of those in high places, not only in government, but also in industry and academia.

There is a constant parade of experts selling us their ideas on improving this part of the system or that, all backed by graphs, charts and statistics. We all see the audio-visual aids, and we understand at least parts of the presentation. But there is something lacking.

We still have our opinions, based on all the information we absorb, both from the experts and from our own experiences in life. It is incredible to most Americans why our leaders in all areas are so unable to cope with our problems in this country, in spite of the fact that they have access to information and resources that are unavailable to the general public.

Still the excuses abound from the power centers of America. We cannot cure the problems because of the civil rights of those who are causing them, or because of the global market, or because of our alliances, or because of the Constitution, or because of the cost. There are so many excuses for failure of leadership.

And where do our leaders find their excuses? In the same places they found the expert advice and information, Washington, D.C., New York, Los Angeles, London, Paris, Tokyo, all the cultural and power centers of the coasts and the world. Surely, there must be something worthwhile in middle America. There must be people in the Midwest with opinions worth noting. We are not fools, out here in the hinterland.

I have felt for three dozen years that our leaders need to listen more to the average normal American. We have views based on what we see and hear, and on our experiences as Americans coping with the daily problems in life, that can be helpful to our leaders in forming new solutions.

At the same time, this work might give some comfort to average Americans "on the bottom", who have always felt they were alone in having real opinions and in being ignored by the power structure.

Average Americans should know they are not alone, that there are millions of us, and that we all have opinions. Our opinions are just as important and sometimes more valid than those of the experts with their statistical backup materials.

Our feelings are based on the experience of real life as well as factual information from surveys and laboratory tests. Besides, our leaders have tried their ways and failed miserably. Why not listen to the common people in America? They can hardly do worse.

After all, it was the average people who pioneered, settled, tamed and built this country to what it is today. Rarely was it exceptional leadership that did the job. Most of the time, when progress was made, it was made by the common, average, ordinary American.

That is what I am, and that is what this work is about —- the opinions of the average middle American on the issues facing us as we make our way through the twenty-first century. I hope it proves to be useful, both to leaders who may find it a helpful tool in reaching our goals as a nation, and to those other average Americans who need to be reassured that they are not alone, and that others share their concerns and attitudes.

In the pyramid that is American society, there are more of us at the base than at the peak of leadership. There are more of us sharing the view from the bottom than from the top. Based on numbers, therefore, it is a view closer to most Americans. If we can learn more about each other, as Americans, and if we can learn to share and to care about one another, then the View from the Bottom will become vision.

Steven L. Kyer

THE VIEW FROM THE BOTTOM

The object of government in peace and in war is not the glory of rulers or of races, but the happiness of the common man.

William Beveridge 1879-1963

British Economist

It is the norm today in America to find countless books and articles exposing the views of the high-placed and the powerful. After all, they are in a position to observe all the facts pertaining to the crucial issues of our day, and that, together with their obvious influence on events, makes their opinions and observations interesting to the man or woman on the street. Moreover, there is an insatiable appetite among the general public these days for information about our government, the economy, defense, public safety, health care, education, and on and on. These published opinions, therefore, fill a need for the people of this country and others; a need to know and understand the events affecting their lives.

But these observations of the powerful do not offer a complete or thorough comprehension of an American society operating in the twenty-first century. What is missing is not a deeper, more technical expose, but a broader view based on the experiences of the average American, trying to deal with and cope with a complex society and its various components, without the advantage of the confidence and control that comes with high position, where events can be influenced. What is missing is the view from the bottom, so to speak.

The events of the day look so different to somebody just reading the daily paper or catching the evening news on television or viewing the latest on a PC. When a local plant shuts down, the plant manager may be disturbed at having to lay off dependable workers, who might be loyal employees of many years. But the office manager who is losing her job will have a slightly more difficult time adjusting to her own loss of income and the lack of control over events affecting her life and her family. The production workers, too, must now suffer the pains of unemployment, and, at their various ages and stages of life, seek new career paths.

And, what about the local businesses which depended on their contracts with the plant? With their business down they, too, may have to terminate employees. And what of the local officials who depend on the taxes paid by the plant and its employees to provide services to the community? And the schools must perhaps curtail some of the educational opportunities provided to the children in the community.

People in all of these situations must see an event from different perspectives and cope with it in different ways according to their positions and the view from which each observes the event. These views are the most important in assessing the preparation of the American public to move through this century. To affect public opinion in order to make the necessary changes in the various parts of our social structure, we must attend critical issues with an eye that is not only technically competent, but also culturally seated. The politician, like any technician, is quite capable in the field of politics, thus politics is played very well in Washington and the various state capitols.

But most politicians have limited understanding in areas of education, health care, economics and the myriad of complex fields and associated issues facing society today. Furthermore, they are insulated from most of the difficulties facing average Americans by their generous pensions, health care programs and assorted benefits and perks arising from their high offices. To comprehend well the problems in education, turn to the student, the teacher, the parent, the school administrator or any of those who deal with those particular problems regularly. For a better understanding of the real issues involving our economy, look no further than the average housewife or any other consumer. Or for another slant, check with a small business owner. For a ring side seat at the fight over better, more affordable health care, talk to a patient, a doctor, a pharmacist or a nurse. Four different accounts will arise on the pitfalls of retaining or changing the current system. But all four will be more valid than the political view.

In all these cases, however, one opinion stands out as the most important, yet least considered—- that of the average ordinary, tax-paying, hard working, product and service buying and voting consumer. Tina Taxpayer; Joe Sixpack; Charlie Consumer. Whatever we call him or her, the person supplying the most valid view from within our society is the average member of our society.

We on the bottom of the American social order have our own views of the world we live in; the world our nation leads. We have opinions on the problems facing other peoples and the role the United States should play in helping to resolve them.

Threats to the environment, the benefits and difficulties of space research and exploration, and adequate nourishment and health care for all humans are global problems and should be addressed as such, although with significant leadership from the United States. America has an important role to play in the family of nations, and we, on the bottom, must judge our leaders on their ability to exercise our leadership.

As for other leaders of the world, they, too, are expected to contribute their skills to improve the overall condition of the human species. Americans have opinions on these various leaders, some good and some not so good, based on the information we see and hear about them. Many have made lasting impressions on us.

Leaders in every country point to a global market today to explain any problems in their own national economic spheres. Is there such an animal as a global economy? What relationship does it share with the American economy? What great or small effects do they have on each other? Economics is a dry topic to most Americans, but we still have opinions on free trade zones, tariffs, protectionism, and anything else that has an ultimate impact on our own pocketbooks. It is necessary, then, that we take a look at the global economy and the American economy as well through the eyes of an average American.

The average American, too, will be a subject of examination. Who is this person? What has created the average American? Is there a monolithic entity such as the average American, or are we a collection of very different persons and groups? What events have shaped the America of the first quarter of the Twenty-first Century? What has happened to the traditional family in America? How can we resolve the problems of racism, child abuse, child support enforcement and abortion in America? How do Americans perceive the Feminist and Gay

Rights movements?

What about the other societal problems facing us as a nation? How can we return our education system to the success it knew as an institution in the middle of the last century? Why has it fallen, and what can we do to eliminate the problems that face the system today? Can the schools overcome the problems created by the family and by society in general? We will see the problems of our schools through the eyes of those who are paying for them, and who feel the value received does not match the money spent.

The same might be said of health care in the United States. Many on the bottom see a national health care system with a top flight calculator, but no heart. Why is the United States one of only two developed countries that do not provide guaranteed health care to all its citizens? Why do we seem to be paying enough to finance such a universal system without having one? In what other areas are we, as a nation, suffering because of this lack of a national system? The average American has ideas on these questions, but probably has even more questions. Is the Affordable Care Act the answer or just another problem? Or could it be just one step closer to the real solution?

Another question in the minds of many on the bottom concerns our sense of values in modern America. Not only do we see the decline of the family in America and poor health and education systems, but there is a sad system of values in our country today. Who are the heroes of our children, and why? Why do entertainers and athletes make more than our teachers or even our doctors? Who has allowed this disintegration of character in our youth, and are our young alone in this lack of character? In an era that included the altruistic sixties, the "me-generation" seventies and the greedy eighties, we on the bottom still have some ideas on how we became what we are and how we might return to what we were.

What we have become has affected our national character, and that has, in turn, affected all aspects of our culture. It is evident even in our legal system. A system that used to insure order in our society and balance wrongs, intentional and unintentional, has become one that is abused regularly by those who would seek gain at the expense of the weak, and disorder at the expense of us all.

The guard of our freedom and our protection against intrusive government now, instead, protects the destroyers, abandons the victims and opens the gate of disintegration to the institutions most vital to the stability and growth of our society. Today, those of us on the bottom are the least protected by our judicial system. We will examine this decline in our system of justice, and the other two branches of government that seem uninterested in checking it.

Of course, the other two branches of government are composed principally of politicians. In a nation such as ours, founded and built on the distrust of political institutions, it is understandable that there would be widespread disenchantment, even today, with those we trust to run the machinery of our government.

We, on the bottom, share with our ancestors this distrust. We have seen nothing in modern politicians, as a group, that substantially differentiates them from those of earlier generations. We will look at the group we choose to lead us at all levels as well as the structure of our government and even the Constitution we support to protect us. Is it perfect? What would we change in it today? Are all politicians crooked, weak and self-serving? What makes them so? How can we as a people do better?

We on the bottom tend to hold the politicians responsible for the failure of all our other institutions. Even the press is viewed with political eyes by the average American. But, ultimately, we on the bottom hold ourselves responsible, even though we sometimes feel unable to change anything. It is the American spirit that sustains us.

This spirit of America will also be examined, along with the ghosts of all our past mistakes. These ghosts seem to intrude in all our thoughts on how to face our nation's problems. We are haunted by them, and, yet, at the same time, we are buoyed by a spirit that seems unknown to most peoples of the world.

Hence, the perpetual belief that America is somehow a special place in all the world. If it truly is, then Americans are a special people with special responsibilities. A special place with special people and special responsibilities must resolve the questions that face them in preparing for a new century. If this work does not offer all the answers, perhaps it can at least provide some of the questions.

A bit of background at this point might help to define the coming remarks and their validity based on their author. Trained originally to teach foreign languages, the author is a retired multiple-line independent insurance agent (that is one who sells all lines of insurance). He was married to a teacher, who taught children with learning disabilities. Together they have a son with a business degree, who works for an oil and gas company, and a daughter with degrees in political science and public administration. She is the human resources director for a university hospital. She is also married to a lobbyist. They have one son.

The author was politically active in the local community, having served on two city councils and in various positions in his political party. He might best be described as a political moderate, having views that could be classified as liberal on some issues and conservative on others.

Having served in public office, the author has great respect for the true public servant, who really wants to improve the status and standard of living for those dependent on his good judgment, and little regard for those too busy feathering nests to attend to the needs of the people who elected them. There are many of each, and an informed public should keep "throwin' 'em out 'til we get a good one."

We, in America, are both blessed and plagued by a constant barrage of discussions of issues by armies of experts from Washington, New York, Los Angeles, London, Paris and around the world. So, it is with a critical eye and harsh judgment that the issues of our day will be reviewed in the view of one on the bottom.

In each area questions will be asked and answers attempted from the position of those of us who must most directly live with the consequences. How does it affect us in its present state? Can we change it? Should we change it? How can we best change it? We will explore the heavy problems from a position beneath the weight of the difficulties themselves. Instead of the superficial pontifications of the so-called experts on the talk shows or the columnists in the newspapers and magazines, we will instead examine the view from the bottom.

THE WORLD

We must build a new world, a far better world —- one in which the eternal dignity of man is respected.

President Harry S. Truman, April 23, 1945

Radio address to the delegates at the opening

of the United Nations conference in San Francisco

It is said that the things that concern the average person in America are those closest to home, be they government, environment or the economy. That is at the very least a debatable assertion, but the truth probably lies somewhere close to it. Perhaps, if distance reduces passion, a view of the world as a whole might be clearer than one of situations closer to home.

Let us, therefore, take a look at the state of the world today and the place the U.S. holds among all the nations. As the acknowledged leader of the world, the United States is in a position to influence many events which have consequences at home.

Even though the U.S. is the only superpower left in the world, we cannot do everything, and we must not dominate the rest of the world, nor could we. There really is a new world order, but what is it?

Where once the U.S. and Soviets had to solve regional conflicts jointly with few others involved, what system exists today to resolve local wars. How can the world solve the problems of famine, disease and poverty, and what role does the United States have?

11

How can we prevent the extinction of whole species of life on this planet? How can we protect the destruction of our environment? Why is the state of health of any people on this earth less than the best it can be, and what can be done to bring good health care to all people?

How can we best use the talents of the whole world to explore and exploit space technology? And what can the world do to rid itself of the scourge of terrorism. These are the principal issues we will see in this chapter through the eyes of those on the bottom in America.

One of the most serious of the roles the U.S. plays on the international level is that of leader of the free world. Unfortunately, all too often in the past that has made us the global policeman.

Since World War II we have had military personnel stationed all over the world, from Germany to Korea to the Phillipines to Bosnia to Iraq and Afghanistan. We were the bulk of the defense against the spread of communism. We had to stave off establishment of leftist dictatorships. Sometimes we actually supported rightist dictatorships in order to prevent leftist ones. Our image in many other lands suffered from such poor judgment.

Because of the intensity of Washington's commitment to halting communism, we defended the West against the Soviet threat of world dominance. We also bore the cost almost exclusively for the maintenance of the gigantic defense establishment necessary for a mission of such proportions.

We had to help poor little West Germany and poor little Japan rebuild. Most Americans supported helping these former enemies get back on their feet. But at some point resentment began to grow to the continued international welfare to countries, who were rebuilt and prospering.

For many years Germany and Japan have been strong enough to defend themselves, even before the fall of the Soviet empire. At the very least they should have been required to reimburse the U.S. for the expense of maintaining our military forces in their countries. And not just part of the expense, but all of it, one hundred percent, should have been paid to us.

The continued subsidization of countries that are perfectly capable of attending to their own needs with their own resources merely exacerbates economic problems in the United States. Money saved by Germany and Japan on Defense is used to subsidize their own industries with government support, allowing them an unfair edge in competing with U.S. firms. This ultimately affects our trade balance and, worse causes job losses in America. We will look deeper into the economic problems related to this area at a later point.

We certainly need a sound defense system for our own security, and we need a certain level of international police work done in order to protect the world from little brush fires which might grow into larger disputes. But it is not only unnecessary, but unwise as well, for the U.S. to be the police department for the whole world.

First no nation should hold that much power over so many other peoples. Such a system would be a constant invitation to abuse. Politicians with their own agendas would involve us regularly in every disagreement around the globe, regardless of the need for intercession, and regardless of any desire of any of the parties involved for our help.

The best example is right in the center of the Middle East – Iraq. Foolish leadership led us into a war that was unnecessary for goals that were unclear at best. Now we are mired in a spreading nightmare, that will only be solved by the deaths of many people, including some of our own.

The people of the United States do not desire such a role for this nation, nor do we want to pay for it. We know we will bear the cost, since we have borne the cost of most world police work for the past half century.

Our national debt is over seventeen trillion dollars and growing. Most, if not all, of that debt can be traced to the enormous expenditures for military forces around the globe. It is time for the other advanced nations of the world to assume their fair share of the cost of maintaining order.

We cannot continue to saddle our grandchildren with debt nobody wants to amortize. There is an obvious and more suitable successor to the role of policing the world——the United Nations.

Recently, the U.N. has begun to grow into the role it should have played all along. Even though the U.S. was the prime player most recent Middle East actions, it was the U.N. and its members who made the decisions and, ultimately, acted on them. Now, the whole world knows that the U.N. can and should be the focal point of international cooperation.

More recently, the five nations that joined with us in the Iran negotiations showed that great nations with different interests can join together in pursuit of goal for the whole world. Germany, Russia, China, Britain and France held together with America to achieve an agreement many thought impossible.

But even the U.N. is plagued with division and misuse. Many in the U.S. do not support the U.N. and want our funding to stop or at least be diminished. And there are those in other countries who stop or sabotage productive efforts by the U.N. to suit their own agendas. Russia is a principle culprit in that regard. Its harassment of former members of the Soviet Union goes unabated by the U.N. because of Russia's veto power in the Security Council.

The unconscionable failure of the U.N. and, for that matter, all the nations of the world, but especially the U.S. and Europe, resulted in the slaughter of innocent noncombatant people in the former Yugoslavia.

First in Croatia and then in Bosnia atrocities were committed by all sides, but mostly by Serbia, while the world looked on wringing its hands. The failure of other nations, especially the European Community, who stood by watching this horrible human tragedy, only reminded us that we as a species have learned little from the Holocaust.

Finally, the U.S. and NATO took separate action and ended that travesty. But we are repeating the mistakes elsewhere. Georgia and Ukraine both have suffered at the hands of Russia, while the world does little more than sanctions. And those are effective mainly in the long run.

Where are the Muslim nations when the Bosnians and Chechnya are defending their homes? They are always ready to fight Israel out of hate, but they seemed reluctant to fight for Bosnian and Chechen Muslims out of love or just plain decency. It is ironic that the despised Judeo-Christian nations (the "Great Satan" U.S.) were expected to solve the problem, and well they should. We must be the most severe judges of ourselves and our actions or our failure to act.

In the 1920's and 1930's, Soviet dictator Josef Stalin allowed or caused the deaths of millions (some estimates run as high as ten million) of Kulaks in the forced collectivization of farms throughout the Soviet Union. Because of the closed media and other information sources in the Soviet Union at that time, little of the world knew of these horrible actions, and those who knew were not heeded.

Then came Adolph Hitler and the most despicable campaign of intentional genocide in the history of the human race. Today leaders at every level in every nation of the world decry the Holocaust, but at the time the "Final Solution" was being carried out, the world feigned ignorance, because it was easier than facing the truth and taking the actions necessary to stop it.

Now leaders of the world claim they would never condone such a thing again. And, yet, the "killing fields" of Cambodia in the 1970's brought little more than mild protest from a world preoccupied with conflicts around the globe at that time.

And, now, once again we as a species face the same haunting question of stopping the outrageous slaughter of innocent fellow human beings. Have we yet learned as a race? And what about

America? Where is the leadership we can and should use? ISIS is a plague in the Middle East.

In a case like this, how can the U.S. ignore the suffering and wait for the rest of the world to make up its mind to act. We have the influence to provoke action. We can and must arouse the neighbors there. Turkey, Egypt, Saudi Arabia and Jordan have more than a million troops under arms and available.

We let it happen in Darfur for much too long. But, of course, there is no oil under Darfur. Is economic interest the only interest we have in the rest of the human race. There is a certain cynicism among those of us on the bottom in the U.S., that those in power in this country are so closely tied to the moneyed interests through their lobbyists and that those moneyed interests determine our national posture throughout the world. Perhaps it is time we as a nation renewed our commitment to principles on which the United States of America was founded.

It is time for the U.S. to lead the rest of the world to take action to stop once and for all the unacceptable abuse of human beings all over the world, and the best place to start at this time is the Middle East. This is the proper role for the U.N. and for the European Community. The U.S. must use its influence to prod them into assuming their responsibilities.

Those responsibilities include the resolution of conflicts among various parts of the former Soviet Union. Georgia has differences with Russia. The Ukraine has a mini civil war that has already drawn in Russia. Russian troops seem to be involved in disrupting former members of the Soviet Union, especially if they seek stronger ties with western Europe.

These are all problems the U.N. was designed to resolve. The time has come for the United Nations to fulfill the dream of its founders, that it would be a forum for resolving disputes among nations and avoid war and suffering. The United States as the most powerful and most influential member should be the prime mover toward that end.

Of course, there is a problem with the use of veto by permanent members. Russia and China use it often to thwart any moves by America that seem counter to their own best interests. And we do the same. It might be time for the entire U.N. to review its charter, perhaps limiting the use of that veto.

But war is not the only cause of suffering in the world. Famine, disease and poverty contribute far more to the pain of the human race. The United States cannot alleviate the suffering of the world alone. We cannot be the pharmacy and health research facility for the whole world.

Most medical research in this country seems to be funded by charitable giving. And we seem to have more research of this kind in America than anywhere else. If we as a species are to defeat the threats of afflictions like cancer and AIDS, we must do it together. And it must be a concerted effort involving not just those, kind enough or affluent enough to donate, but the nations of the earth.

Government spending by all nations according to their resources should be the foundation of medical research, since it is all the peoples of all nations that will reap the benefits. Cooperative effort, perhaps through the World Health Organization, can accomplish much more toward ending the scourge of disease, than the costly individual research conducted by the various national efforts, often duplicating work and wasting valuable money and time.

How much of the world's human resources have been lost to disease. How many potential leaders in all areas of human endeavor have been lost, depriving all of the benefit of genius, of talent, of strength and of love? Cooperation among nations would be more productive and far less costly to all of us.

That air of cooperation seems to be growing in one area, the environment. It seems the world began to notice that we were abusing and depleting the one resource that we cannot survive without, and the one that is absolutely finite—-the planet Earth.

International cooperation seems to be having an effect on this abuse.

We are attempting to halt the destruction of whole species of animal life, many of which are on the endangered list and bordering on extinction even now. Some unfortunately have been lost, but many have been and are being saved by this unique joint effort by many nations with many different sets of priorities.

We all agree we must take care of what we have as human kind. And if this kind of cooperation is possible in this area, it can be achieved on other levels as well.

Climate change has been noted and accepted as fact by all peoples, with the exception of a few with their heads buried in the sand. Unfortunately, many Republicans and other conservatives right here in the U.S. choose to reject the consensus of 97% of all scientists around the world. If they don't see the problem, they don't have to act, or to spend.

One prime activity that cries out for a united effort to benefit the entire world is space research and exploitation. Note the word exploitation. Space exploration is certainly a fascinating and important facet in the various space programs, but space exploitation is most immediately crucial to providing the kind of benefits needed to justify the large expenditures required to achieve orbital levels, where most research on human problems can be done.

There are so many research projects which can provide new products and methods in areas such as medicine and manufacturing, and these improvements then result in improved standards of living for countless millions, perhaps billions of men, women and children around the globe.

The International Space Station has proven that cooperative efforts of many nations can yield fantastic scientific information. That in turn becomes new advancement in medicine and industry that benefits all of us. Further development of new space vehicles for deliveries of supplies and occupants to the station is crucial. This will also advance human efforts to reach further into space exploration.

There are many other serious issues facing the world community, and a complete discussion of all of them would take volumes. This is not intended to be a thorough study of all such topics, but one more subject deserves attention —- terrorism.

This sinister plague has been a blight on the human race throughout history, but in recent years it has assumed new forms. Whether terrorists are highjacking a plane, holding innocent people hostage or bombing public places to harm or frighten those nearby, their activities threaten the orderly settlement of human differences. These acts have become so numerous and commonplace today that people from all nations must fear for their safety at home and abroad.

The September 11, 2001, attack on the World Trade Center focused the attention of the world on this disease infecting humankind. The wanton killing of thousands of innocent people shows the terrorists have no love or feeling for other human beings. It also sent a striking message to all peoples everywhere.

It is absolutely essential that the civilized world find a solution to end this modern day barbarism. Many innocent people have been killed or maimed by diabolical groups who seek to impose their ideologies or sometimes just their will on the rest of the world. On many occasions the identity of individual terrorists is known by government authorities.

When this is the case, perhaps their families should be rounded up and held to exchange as ransom for hostages. Or maybe authorities should threaten the safety of terrorists' family members if other innocent people are harmed. This may seem a harsh method, but, if innocent people are going to be harmed or killed, let it be those cherished by the terrorists. If they believe this will be the case, they may decide against such violence.

There are those who will say we must not allow ourselves to stoop to the level of such criminals, or that such actions would make us no better than those we seek to stop. The war against terrorism is just that —- a war.

During World War II, many tons of bombs were dropped on Cologne, Dresden and other cities full of civilian inhabitants, the large majority of whom must have been innocent noncombatants. But this was necessary to defeat the Third Reich, just as dropping the bomb on Hiroshima, though surely a tragic taking of innocent life, just as surely brought an end to the war in the Pacific.

If the world is determined to end terrorism as a method of international or national policy, then it must resolve to take whatever action is necessary to win this fight. And it is obvious that the United States is the only nation with the diplomatic currency to bring about a consensus for action.

The United States has been and must continue to be a leader in this and all other areas of world cooperation. This world doesn't need more Americas, but it does need the leadership of our America to help all the other nations become the best they can be for their individual peoples.

Each nation has its own character and personality. Each has priorities and goals that reflect the aspirations of its people. They do not need us to set our goals for them to achieve. But perhaps the light that is America can help them find their best destiny as we have done and continue to do.

We cannot be the world's policeman, but maybe we can help the United Nations police the world. We cannot be doctor to each country with health problems, but we may be the midwife at the birth of that people's own ability to cope. We cannot shuttle the whole world into space, but we might possibly be the booster that propels our neighbors on this planet to join us there.

We cannot save the world from itself in any theater of human involvement, but we are in a unique position in human history to influence all our fellow nations to join together in a journey to a new and better world, right here on earth.

THE GLOBAL MARKET

No nation was ever ruined by free trade.

Benjamin Franklin (1706-1790)

"It's the economy—-stupid!" That was the catch-phrase of the 1992 U.S. Presidential election campaign. But it might just as well be the simplest description of what ails most of the people on this planet. Countries on almost every continent are plagued by hunger and desperation.

Even in the most developed nations there are homeless, jobless, hopeless people scattered among the affluent. Why, in this age of accelerated human achievement are there any at all who are left out, left behind or just left by a human society with eyes so trained on what is ahead that we cannot notice those who are not surviving today much less looking to the future? There are whole peoples who are starving; who have no livelihood, no way to care for themselves and their children.

Let's look at the so-called global market from the bottom. The global market is cited for every economic problem facing the average American. Our leaders blame it for inflation, recession, the falling of the value of the dollar, slow production, job losses and just about anything else that can affect our pocketbooks.

That is, unless it is something good. If jobs increase, income goes up or the economy in the U.S. is flourishing, it is because of the positive actions in Washington.

But what is the global economy, and what part do we really play in it as a nation? What real impact does it have on us? When we help other nations, do we hurt our own economy, and are we really helping them. Is free trade really free? Who benefits from free trade zones? Americans have ideas on these issues. We read. We study. We observe. And what do we think?

Throughout history whole nations are known to have perished due to famine, natural disasters or war. Why should we be concerned today about the same fate facing hundreds of millions of modern day inhabitants of our world? The answer is—- Communication! Our predecessors had an excuse.

They did not know in most instances what was happening to their fellow human beings far, far away. By the time our ancestors found out about anything important happening in the world, the event was long over. It was history. They could not be held accountable for most of what took place in the world, good or bad.

We, however, have the benefit of modern communications. Today information travels instantaneously anywhere in the world. We know about great accomplishments, natural disasters or human failure almost as they take place.

And, if we allow suffering to continue unchecked anywhere around the globe, we must accept a guilt that no generation before us has had to carry. We have it within our power as a species to alleviate pain and suffering among all peoples to a degree never before imagined. Today we truly are our "brother's keeper." We cannot hide from such a responsibility.

So, why, then, does hunger persist? Why does senseless war continue? Why are there homeless people? Why does disease spread in some parts of the world while a cure exists? These are the questions that should haunt everyone in the developed world.

Why do medicines sit on shelves and sometimes deteriorate, while there are those who are suffering and dying for lack of the same medicines? Why is food destroyed in some places in order to preserve market prices, while countless millions throughout the world are dying of starvation?

While we in America and other so-called developed countries are preparing for the twenty-first century, many in this same world are living in conditions more common in the seventeenth century. It is time to pause in our quest for a grand future and reflect on the plight of many who are struggling to cope with today.

We in the United States have in the past attempted to provide assistance to less developed areas of the world. There are the Peace Corps, Aid for International Development and many other agencies and programs which have been established over the years to direct resources to those in need of help.

These are noble efforts, and they tend to be consistent with the idea that people are better off if they learn to care for themselves. In other words, "Give a man a fish, and he eats for a day. Teach a man to fish, and he will eat for a lifetime." We have of course also provided a "fish" for today, while we have tried to teach "fishing". Then, why isn't it working?

Trillions of dollars have been spent by this country and others to help the less advanced peoples of the world, and yet there seems to be little progress in many areas. Americans, especially, are growing weary of this international welfare system that seems to perpetuate dependence on handouts.

Why can't these peoples, who have lived for centuries in most cases in their own lands do what a nation of immigrants did in a land they first had to take and then tame. Pioneers in this country left the relative safety of the eastern seaboard of America and headed west with little knowledge of the land they were entering or of the circumstances they would face. Yet, through hard work, endurance and perseverance, they succeeded in building the greatest nation on earth.

They created a system of self-government that is a model for the whole world. They built an economy that for all its troubles is among the strongest in the world. And they forged a nation out of many disparate peoples from all over the globe that serves as a shining example of what human cooperation can achieve.

Many Americans find it difficult to understand why other peoples cannot accomplish what our own forebears did. Can no one else in the world exert the effort and commitment that proved so successful here?

Notwithstanding the societal problems that exist in America today, this country is still the envy of the world. That is not to say all people everywhere would rather live in the United States. Most in the world, however, would like their own lands to fair as well as the U.S., and many thousands immigrate legally and illegally to this country every year.

They come for freedom; they come for health; they come to reunite families. They come for many reasons, but most come for opportunity. It's the economy. Not only is America's economy among the strongest in the world, it is one of the easiest in which to blend and to succeed. For a long time there was no real competition to the U.S. in world trade.

But now the world is changing rapidly, most significantly in political and economic areas. Looking up from the bottom in America, we see a European Community that has come into its own prominence as an economic zone. It might prove to be the most important economic development in the world to date.

Nations that have fought so many wars among themselves over the centuries are working together for common growth; and possibly even someday forging a real political union. Such achievements would not have been thought possible just forty or fifty years ago. But if Europe is breaking down barriers, it is not alone.

Japan is achieving great success at forging economic agreements with China, South and North Korea, Taiwan, and other growing economies of the Asiatic community. China is experimenting with a market economy and took a giant leap forward when it took control of Hong Kong, and integrated the two systems. China has even established trade agreements with Taiwan, its arch-enemy. Together, the nations of Asia are extremely competitive in the world marketplace. Their resources, both natural and human, are formidable.

But Asia must also deal with the squalor that exists in many areas there. Places like Vietnam, having emerged from the devastation of more than three decades of war, and Burma, with its political instability, are struggling to provide an adequate environment for even a domestic economy to grow.

India, which has a Western style democracy, provides little hope for so many of its people for a better life. Disease and deprivation are commonplace in these and many other countries in this part of the world. The average person in the U.S. has little comprehension of the situations in these lands that allow such conditions to persist. It is obvious that something must be done; something must be changed. But what?

The same holds true for South America. The abundance of resources clearly indicates a prominent place at the world economic table, and yet the nations of this area are lacking in providing many of the basic needs of their people, especially in rural areas. These countries were settled and dominated for centuries by Europeans.

Why, then, are they not enjoying the same prosperity that thrives in Europe. Their languages, their cultural ties and their social systems are derived from their former "mother" countries. There would seem to be a natural trading block among them to further the long range development of all. And yet the most prosperous industry in this part of the world is the illegal drug business.

The peasant farmers make more money growing plants that provide drugs than coffee. The drug lords have armies that are well paid to defend them against comparatively weak government forces. These ineffective and sometimes undemocratic governments spend so much of their financial resources fighting illegal drugs, that there is little left to help the legitimate economy to thrive.

Corruption among government officials adds to the problem, along with the lack of democratic traditions in most of the nations of South America, although that last twenty years has seen a great deal of improvement in this regard.

No nation on earth is going to provide an economic system built on drug trafficking that benefits all its people. Only the drug lords and the crooked officials will gain. And, even they will export most of the profits to the distributors in the user nations.

One can only hope that with international cooperation to stamp out the narcotics trade, these poor nations will be able to turn their attentions to building another economic trading block to benefit their peoples and other parts of the world as well. The United States has provide substantial help over the past several decades to try to stamp out the drug trafficking.

Africa, like South America, seems to have so many problems to overcome, it may be some time before it can turn to its various economies. Political upheaval is so common that when one spot calms down, another flares up.

Egypt appeared for a long time to be the most stable nation in all of Africa, but Islamic fundamentalists have caused chaos for years there, and even had the chance to promote an Islamic republic for Egypt. It was such a failure, that public demonstrations brought it down, and they have elected another former military chief to run the country again.

When South Africa finally achieved a non-racial system, its resources made it easily the most viable on the continent. The basic structures in South Africa make it more like European countries. When Nelson Mandela was elected President, the country took a giant leap forward, and it has since emerged as the economic leader of Africa. Such success and prosperity might spread throughout the area bringing a twentieth century standard of living to countless millions.

But before that, we on the bottom in America will continue it seems to watch famine and war take a toll in places like Somalia,

Sudan, Chad, Namibia, and so many other nations in what at one time was a mere colonial resource for Europe.

The colonies, one by one, were given independence by their European sponsors with little preparation for self-government and little understanding of democracy or the principles of economic survival. With the exception of Zimbabwe and South Africa, the nations of Africa have always had governments controlled by native populations ill-prepared by their former colonial masters.

One might say that Algeria, because of its former status as a legitimate Department (State) of France has some basic understanding of self-government, but Egypt and South Africa are the only nations in Africa which were actually prepared by their colonial master, England, to be an independent, self-governing democracy.

And, because of this, it would seem, those two appear to have a fairly stable and viable economy, despite their lack of any rare or otherwise valuable natural resources (unless we count the diamond mines in South Africa). Perhaps, with encouragement from the rest of the world and an evolution of democratic tradition, the other nations of Africa can learn from these two and someday take their place at the economic table of world prosperity.

Possibly the brightest economic spot in the southern hemisphere is the area of Australia and New Zealand. These two defy the trend of South America and Africa and seem to prosper among the economies of the world. They have European traditions and economic ties as well as beneficial trade with the nations of Asia and North America.

Stable democratic governments are a prime factor in this success, but by and large it is the people that make their systems work. They share some characteristics with the people of North America. They have carried on the traditions they brought from Europe, especially their form of government.

But, they also have the industry and social stability to use the resources available to achieve their economic goals and provide the best possible standard of living for everyone. The average American considers the people of Australia and New Zealand to be very much like "us".

Next to us lie Canada and Mexico, one thriving with us and the other striving to join us. For many years we have had an almost borderless relationship with Canada, with trade a travel back and forth between us such an everyday thing that most don't notice that we are, indeed, different countries.

The traditions and cultural background of our two nations together with our common heritage as former British colonies have linked us in what most Americans consider a common destiny. We appear to enjoy most of the same basic democratic freedoms and similar standard of living.

Mexico on the other hand has been the poor relative in North America. Lacking the common bonds that exist between Canada and the United States, Mexicans have always exhibited in the eyes of the average American a combination of envy and resentment toward us. Mexico has never had what Americans would call a real democratic tradition.

One party has controlled Mexico for more than a century, and the average Mexican seems to be at the mercy of corrupt officials who drain the treasury and use the system for themselves and their friends. The picture we have of the average Mexican is one of a poor powerless individual who faces little hope of economic prosperity for his family or for the future of the next generation.

Americans even fear travelling to Mexico because of a justice system that is internationally suspect and the corruption that is known to exist among Mexican bureaucrats. That reputation has cost Mexico considerable tourism and business investment.

However, in recent years some progress has been made between our two governments to encourage more travel and investment in Mexico by Americans. The Mexicans have rooted out some of the more dishonest officials especially among law enforcement agency personnel, and they have been very successful at promoting their readily available cheap labor to American companies seeking to lower production costs. The resulting expansion of American investment in Mexico has caused concern among U.S. labor unions.

The establishment of the North American Free Trade Agreement (NAFTA) among Canada, Mexico and the United States has stirred considerable debate over the adverse effects of cheap Mexican labor on U.S. workers and their jobs, many of which moved south of the border.

Environmentalists have also raised serious questions about lax Mexican laws on pollution by various industries of air and water resources. Mexico is considered notoriously lax in making laws to protect the environment and ineffective in enforcing those laws that do exist. But, the bright spot in this picture has been the expected reduction in illegal immigration from Mexico to the United States.

But the illegal immigrants are still a cause for great debate, especially among conservatives here. Most illegals come across the border in search of jobs and work for very low wages to earn enough to take back home to care for their families in the very depressed Mexican economy. Most of us bottom level Americans worry greatly over the adverse effects of all the proposed free trade arrangements, but we hope for a better outcome than we have come to expect from the politicians on high who have made them.

The North American Free Trade Agreement (NAFTA) is typical. It was negotiated by two different administrations from two different parties, and still there are a great many in the United States who point at all the lost jobs and other negative impacts. From organized labor unions to environmental groups to civil rights advocates, there is great conviction that the United States has suffered while Mexico and big businesses continue to reap a tremendous harvest.

Even though side agreements were signed to address these concerns, the opposition has remained steadfast. The strongest argument against NAFTA, besides the job loss and environment problems (supposedly solved by the side agreements) is the case against Mexico's civil rights record.

Opponents argue that we should have waited on any free trade agreement with Mexico until that country brought the lot of its people up to our level and the level of Canada. In other words, when the Mexican people are free, then they are ready for free trade.

Proponents argued just as strongly that NAFTA would not only bring new jobs to Americans through new markets, but it would bring prosperity to Mexicans and with it the civil liberties they should have. Unfortunately, those benefits have not come as quickly as the new jobs. And pay levels and benefits are still on the horizon.

With the proliferation of trade agreements, trade zones and economic communities the world seems to have entered a new era in human economic cooperation. All Americans have heard the term "global economy" for years from politicians and business leaders, who used such terms to excuse the leadership failures in the United States.

Now, finally, it appears there may be some benefits to be achieved for all in such agreements, notwithstanding the environmental and labor cost concerns, if we can only rely on those at the top to execute their obligation to make sure the yield is high and the losses are few. The new markets can and do make a difference, and we are trending toward high increases in jobs that are technical and highly skilled.

And let's also make sure that it is not just the few at the top who reap the harvest. For if these efforts fail it will be, as always, those masses on the bottom who will pay the price for that failure.

AMERICA - A HOUSE DIVIDED

If a house be divided against itself, that house cannot stand.

The Gospel according to St. Mark 3:25

The United States of America is more than just the name of a country. In the minds of average Americans, it is a statement about who we are. Americans as a whole share a romantic vision of the founding and building of our nation. Being an American gives a feeling of pride. But what is America? What is our vision of the creation of what we now call the United States? Are we just united states, or are we also united as a people? Do the things that unite us also divide us? What do we share in common, and what are our differences from within? How can we be so divided on such emotional issues as we face today and remain a united country? Can we overcome our differences? Let's see how one on the bottom views America, where we have been, and where we are going.

The United States today has come full circle. We began as colonies of European giants —- England, France and Spain. We as a people evolved from many groups of immigrants from many foreign lands, who came, saw a rich future compared to what they had left, and who through determination and perseverance conquered a continent and all the adversities it held.

Through two centuries, our forebears spread their culture and their New-World personality into new areas of this hemisphere, building

31

communities, towns and ultimately new States to add to the nation they created from pieces they had taken from their European mother countries and from the Native Americans they found unable to resist this overpowering force of numbers and advanced technology.

This new people created from so many old cultures overcame their differences of backgrounds, nationalities, and attitudes after decades of intermingling and ultimately a Civil War to become what is now the United States of America. It is said that prior to the Civil War our country was referred to by its own people in the plural, that is as "The United States are…" or "The United States,…they…". After the war, however, the reference was always "The United States is…" or "The United States,…it…". We had developed a consciousness of ourselves as one people and one nation. No longer were we just a group of States, but a country like any other in the world, and yet different from all others.

All other nations of the world were formed by people with a more or less common ethnic heritage. They had a natural affinity for each other, borne of a shared ancestry and commonly developed culture. Yet, here was a new entity founded not so much on blood lines or even on bloodshed (although it certainly played a part), but on the concept that ballots were superior to bullets in finding a destiny for our people.

This was perhaps the single most important development in human cultural history. Because of this freedom from tyranny, people flocked to this country from every other in the world, seeking to find a degree of individual success for themselves and for their children, that they could not conceive in their homelands. They felt that in a land that allowed them to determine their own fate without interference from a monarch, an emperor, a dictator or any authority but one they ordained, and one that was accountable to them and their new compatriots, they could grow and flourish.

And flourish they did. Once these Americans, as they were now called, had spread their new country from Atlantic to Pacific, they proceeded to join it with the first real national transportation system, the railroad. Then they united themselves with a continental communication system, the telegraph. With these two momentous events together with the united self-image following the Civil War, America was set to lead the industrial revolution that brought the whole world into the twentieth century that we now herald as the most productive century in history for the betterment of humankind.

Our transportation system developed into the modern system of highways, railways and airports that today is the most advanced in the world. We gave the world the modern automobile, the airplane and the computerized travel system that has made the world so small that there is now nowhere on this planet that is inaccessible.

The telephone and almost every other modern form of communication can be credited to American know-how. And the cell phone, now the standard preferred communication device in most western countries is a direct result of our space program. We can now talk with and be seen by anyone in the world at will and instantaneously. These and many other advances along with the sheer will of the American people made this the most powerful and the most prosperous nation in history.

Americans are justifiably proud of our accomplishments as a people. Most of us believe that God has made this a special place in the world, a place of hope like none found anywhere else on earth. This is certainly not the Garden of Eden, but where else could one born in poverty grow up to become the leader of his country? More than one president has come from a modest or even poor background.

Where else could a Sam Walton have grown from poverty to billionaire? Or a Thurgood Marshall from a poor family to the United States Supreme Court? Or a Barack Obama to President of the United States? And so many others in this country have found success to supplant the meager resources of their families. "Only in America" has become a expression common around the world to describe the opportunity so readily available to many here and so few anywhere else in the world.

If Americans are so justifiably proud, if so many in the world look to America for leadership and opportunity, if this land offers so much to so many, then why is America so often derided by some in other countries, and why is the United States so divided as a people on so many crucial issues today? Why does poverty even exist in such a prosperous nation as this? Is opportunity really still available to everyone here? Is the United States a united people?

President Abraham Lincoln is supposed to have said, quoting the Bible, "A house divided against itself cannot stand." He was referring, of course, to the States and their union, and the Civil War resolved that issue. But did it resolve the larger issue of union of the national psyche, the national soul? If we as a people are to survive as a nation, we will have to resolve the issues that separate us emotionally into camps, into special interest groups.

Unless we can learn to disagree without becoming disagreeable, we cannot truly feel united. Today's America is sharply divided on so many emotional issues. At times, Lincoln's house seems more divided against itself than ever before.

Sometimes we don't even refer to ourselves as Americans. We instead tend to describe ourselves according to which social division we identify with ourselves. We have politicians, magazines, TV shows, radio talk shows and many other social outlets that identify with one group or another. Perhaps "cater to" would be better than "identify with" to describe the relationship of some of these, especially the politicians. They are uniquely vulnerable to the necessity to pay homage to various issue groups, and the number of special interest groups seems to grow almost daily.

Our view from the bottom in America varies according to which of the many groups we belong to at a given time. Older Americans, especially Baby Boomers, those born during the fifteen years following World War II, are apprehensive now that they are reaching retirement. They feel the resentment of the younger generation at having to fund their parents and grandparents in retirement. This "generation gap" may be greater than that between any two generations before.

Probably the most emotional gap between any Americans today is that between certain ethnic or racial groups. African-Americans feel many times that they have been denied a meaningful opportunity to achieve the American dream. Many Hispanic and Native Americans feel the same denial. White Americans on the other hand feel that many minority Americans have not made enough effort to take advantage of the opportunities that are available. They believe they are denied their rights when quotas or affirmative action are used to "level the playing field" for members of minority groups, and they resent encroachment on their "earned opportunity."

As voters, white Americans will soon become a minority, and they feel threatened by the others gaining power in our system. The Republican Party has increasingly become old, white, male and conservative. If they don't increase their share of African-Americans, Hispanics and young women, the party may shrink to irrelevance.

Then there are the strict issue-oriented groups. There seems to be no common ground acceptable to Pro-Choice and Pro-Life advocates in the abortion controversy. Both argue staunchly for all or nothing in this truly emotional debate.

Just as emotionally charged are the Feminist and Gay Rights movements in America today. There is almost a trench warfare mentality in both. The battle lines are drawn, and woe to the politician or institution that takes up with the wrong side. The leaders of the differing sides in these fights are not the compromising types. They demand total allegiance and agreement.

While trends have brought Gay Rights, especially marriage equality to be accepted by the majority, there is still a conservative backlash in some places. Even with legalization, some will never accept that level of equality. Religious zealots are the staunchest opponents.

There are other groups dividing Americans today, some perhaps not as emotionally charged as those already mentioned but no less important to those affected. Labor and management still have sharp differences on the rights of American working men and women as opposed to the meaningful expectations of investors and those charged with realizing business profits.

Many workers in the United States feel that their efforts to care for their families are not important to business management or to political leaders. They, therefore, feel they are sometimes denied the opportunity to provide a better future America should offer their children. Some business managers see government interference and unions as major obstacles to attaining the profitability their investors expect.

And now the wage gap has become a major issue facing our entire economy. While those in the top one percent of earners are making extraordinary advances in income, the poor and especially the middle class have seen continual drops in true income and spending power for several decades. Trickle-down economics has proved to be a mirage. And most wonder where we can look for leadership to right the ship.

Government in America today has achieved a degree of distrust among the average citizens at every level that is in sharp contrast to the personal belief of Americans in the democratic system. Actually, it seems to be the politicians and the bureaucracy that have provoked such distrust.

Americans see government as incompetent, insensitive, unresponsive and out of control. Most today have had at least one bad experience with government in general and many with the bureaucracy before they finish school. It is no wonder that issues like term limitation and balanced budget amendments receive such popular support when put before the voters.

Add to these the divisions over health care availability and education, and the United States of America begins to look like a collection of inert elements which cannot be combined into a useful form. The Affordable Care Act was passed in 2010, and has provided better opportunities for health care for millions, yet opponents still propose dismantling the entire program, with absolutely no alternative proposal.

Moreover, these are only current issues that divide us. There are ghosts of issues past that haunt Americans even today. We do not make a move as a people without considering our national memory. Many of us alive today still have personal memories of the Depression, Korea, Vietnam, the Cold War, 911 and many other traumatic or otherwise impressive events which affected our attitudes toward life and the courses of action we should take as a nation when confronted by choices of consequence.

We on the bottom see not only the world but America and our future as a people through the eyes of those who have experienced the best and the worst. We have seen police actions that were really war. Since World War II, we have been in and out of one war after another all over the world. We seem to be charged with policing countries everywhere, and we have to pay the entire bill. Why must we spend more of our GDP on defense than the rest of the world combined?

We have elected representatives who do not seem to represent us. We have built the finest health care facilities in the world only to see them deny full access to one third of us, although we seem to be closing that gap. We saved the whole world from the tyranny of communism, but saddled ourselves with an insurmountable national debt. We have preserved for ourselves the rights given us as inalienable by our creator, yet we cannot feel safe in our own community or homes. We are haunted by the ghosts of our national past, but long for a future that realizes the American dream for all of us. We see ourselves as a united people, but we are divided into so many emotionally charged groups.

How do we rebuild the bridges between our various factions, especially the Tea Party right and the more liberal left? How do we preserve a balanced two party system, when there is such a legacy of personal hatred toward members of each by the other? Can we breed new politicians and other leaders, who can remain above narrow views of special interests and lobby groups?

How do we overcome the contradiction which is the United States of America? How can we address the divisions in this house, overcome them and insure that the house will remain standing? Can we as Americans draw strength once again from our diversity? In the view of one on the bottom—— Yes!

RACISM

When I was five years old, as I recall, I was outside playing with neighborhood friends one day, when one of the other boys did something, I don't remember what, that made me angry. I called him "nigger", and he hit me. I ran crying for my mother. When she came out, she asked what had happened. I told her that the boy had hit me. She asked him why, and he told her. My mother spanked me and told me never to call anyone that name again because it was a very bad name. I never used the term again. Years later, when I found out I was of Jewish and Cherokee heritages, I understood. It is a hateful word.

Author

Bigotry must be a universal genetic disorder. Science perhaps should search for a bigotry gene, in hope of someday altering it to eliminate this malady from humankind. Why are people prejudiced toward others? Is a stereotype always wrong? Is there no basis for stereotypes? Are only white people bigoted? How can such attitudes affect us as a society? Can they be changed? Is it harmful if they are not changed? What can we do to eliminate the problems that cause bigotry, and the problems that are caused by it?

Every American has views on this subject, and no one person could hope to represent adequately all ideas related to it. Each could, however, attempt to see the problem through the eyes of others in hope of achieving better understanding. Where two sides of an issue are examined, the truth that lies somewhere between them may be discovered.

The most emotionally divisive issue facing Americans today is racism. It seems as if even the most liberally tolerant among us harbor at least some bigoted views toward members of other ethnic or racial groups. Many of these attitudes are subtle, but there are those that are quite open about their distrust or dislike of a particular group or groups.

A few are belligerent; others may be actually militant in their hatred. Although the common perception is that racist attitudes are found mostly among white Americans, there seems to be some bigotry almost uniformly distributed among the various ethnic groups in the United States.

Surely, the number of white bigots is largest, simply because there are more whites in America than any other racial or ethnic group. And there are a great many whites who do not like African Americans, Asian Americans, Hispanic Americans, Native Americans or any other Americans who are not just like themselves.

But that is not to say they are the only bigots here. There are a large number of African Americans who are quite intolerant of whites, resenting what they see as a superior attitude among all whites.

Many Asian Americans resent not only white attitudes they see as arrogant, but also what they perceive as anti-Asian sentiments among other ethnic groups in America. Hispanic and Native Americans have been vexed for quite a long time over what they see as their inferior position in American society.

These views appear irrational in light of the generally adopted attitude of Americans as in the Declaration of Independence that "all men are created equal", but what we feel as patriots and what we feel as individuals are entirely different. A normal person identifies most readily with his family, then with his heritage, then with his country and, finally with human kind in general.

Each needs to feel a pride derived from all four in order, since all four define the individual to some degree. Derision or degradation of any one of the four demeans the individual according to the closeness of the identifying factor, so that insulting the family is the most hurtful and enraging, and berating the human race the least. A person's heritage then is awfully close to family and to self.

So it is not without some justification that members of any minority group might become angered or hurt by the attitudes of those in other groups, especially those in the majority. At the same time some in the majority may feel victimized by social pressures to accept behavior or customs they find at the very least uncomfortable.

Who is right? Who has the correct attitude? Is there any justification for feelings of persecution, intolerance, superiority or, for that matter, inferiority? Each ethnic or racial group can offer sometimes convincing arguments for their beliefs regarding the others. The most visible group claiming discrimination, and, it seems rightfully, is African Americans. And color is the most frequent reason cited.

Anyone who saw the miniseries "ROOTS" had to sense feelings of hatred for most whites depicted in the series. They were the evil strangers who enticed Africans to capture members of other tribes and sell them for trinkets to other whites, who in turn shipped them under inhumane conditions to a young America for sale to in most cases equally subhuman plantation owners.

Even though slavery has existed throughout human history, there seems to be no record of any more barbarous than that in the United States. Slave owners completely discounted the humanity of Africans, and they treated them as mere chattel.

In fact, farm animals were treated better in most cases. No farmer would have considered beating a horse or other farm animal as harshly as some slaves. Of course, farm animals don't run away, because, not being human, they have no sense of the value of freedom.

41

The United States was among the last of the developed countries of the nineteenth century to abolish slavery as a national institution. But even today in the Twenty-first Century, there are those in America who have never accepted the basic notion of human equality. And black Americans feel the pain of such bigotry perhaps more acutely, because of their sense of their own history, and because much of the hatred of whites is expressed so overtly.

The frustration of knowing that many opportunities for education, for jobs, for careers, for housing or just for acceptance at some level being denied because of color or personal heritage infuriates some African Americans so much that they develop an equal intolerance for all whites, who, they feel, have denied them the personal pride that every person deserves.

During the civil rights movement of the 1960s, many white Americans, especially in the north, felt a personal shame at the images they saw on television news shows of police brutality against blacks seeking basic civil rights. Most whites outside the South saw the movement as a just cause and supported it.

Their representatives in Congress reflected as much in the passage of the Civil Rights Act and other legislation to eliminate most of the overt discrimination that had permeated American society since the post-Civil War era. Dr. Martin Luther King, Jr., was an American hero to many non-blacks in this country for his courageous and righteous leadership. Many blacks felt that finally there would be equality for them in American society.

But, unfortunately, bigotry not only has persisted here, but it has grown in some ways. Many white Americans resent the progress made by African Americans, who, they feel, have gained at the expense of whites. When black students are admitted to some schools or classes to increase minority participation, a white student who was not admitted is likely to feel a black student took his place.

When a black employee is hired under an affirmative action plan, an unemployed white probably will feel cut out of a job by a black who is not as qualified. The African American in either case may be well qualified, but that will not assuage the feelings of the white who was unsuccessful in seeking the position.

A black American may feel rightfully that African Americans, as a group, have been denied equal access to the opportunities that have been available to whites since emancipation.

When the slaves were freed, they were given nothing to take with them; no possessions, no training, no education, no jobs, no chance. For a hundred years they were discriminated against openly by school officials, employers, and just about every social institution in America, including the political apparatus.

Whites, even the less qualified and the unqualified got the jobs. Whites got the best schools. Whites got the vote and had the system, especially the judicial and bureaucratic systems, on their side. Black Americans could not go to the best schools or find the best jobs.

Professional careers were unavailable except to a very lucky few. They were routinely denied the vote, and they could count on little justice from the courts, no protection from law enforcement officials and little consideration from government bureaucrats.

Without an education or a substantial job, it was difficult for any African American to provide a basis for the family to prosper, for the children to advance in school or into a better earning position than the parents had. Each generation was relegated to the same rung on the social ladder occupied by parents and grandparents.

Only in recent years has there been a significant opportunity for this generation of African Americans to achieve a great deal more than their parents'. Affirmative action in the eyes of today's African Americans is not social welfare. It is not a quota system. It is not a giveaway program. It is merely a handicap given to even the playing field in order to give an applicant the same chance that would have been available had previous generations had equal opportunities. They don't want a handout; they want the system to be even-handed.

This includes the justice system. African Americans see a law enforcement and judicial system that slaps white offenders on the wrist while beating a black violator over the head. Hence, the reaction to the Rodney King verdict. In the view of many, had Rodney King been white, no such beating by arresting officers would have happened.

This was just one more incident, in which white police officers used brutal and unnecessary force to punish a black suspect. The film shown on national news programs over and over reinforced in the minds of black Americans the second class status they held in the American system of justice, and the first jury verdict reaffirmed that view.

And over the years we have seen more such incidents. More recently, black suspects have been beaten to death and shot to death, even though they were unarmed. A twelve-year-old was shot to death by a police officer in Cleveland while brandishing a toy pistol.

The helpless feeling of so many African Americans in the face of such perceived injustice left them with no way to express their outrage except through violence and destruction. They needed a visible outlet for their frustration. In many communities, riots followed the incidents. Of course, outsiders and criminals take advantage of such situations, causing whites to claim such lawlessness exemplifies black communities. And bigotry grows from such stereotypes.

And the African American community resents that even more. The most visible symbol of the society that seemed to deny them their chance in America was American businesses.

After all, business seems to run this country. Business has access to the political system. Business has all the money. Business denies them jobs and forces them onto welfare, a trap many never escape. In their view businesses may seem to represent all that have denied them the American dream.

Many, especially in the inner cities, cannot afford to own a home and live in sometimes run down rental properties. This is not unique to poor black families, but sometimes it may seem to them that they sustain more of the poverty in this country than any other single group.

Many feel they are not given the police protection in poor black neighborhoods that is provided to more affluent or white areas. As a result they see drug dealers, thieves, arsonists and other criminals victimizing their families and especially their children seemingly unchecked. It is no wonder that African Americans feel their country has abandoned them. And their country is controlled by whites. Should they not hold whites responsible for their plight?

Fortunately, there are organized efforts to improve the lives of African Americans. The most notable is of course the National Association for the Advancement of Colored People. The NAACP has probably done more to benefit African Americans than any other single organization in history. Most of the improvements in the standard of living and, indeed, in the standard of life for the average African American can be traced directly to the activities and the actions of the NAACP.

And others have benefited as well. Many of the achievements of the NAACP have helped Native Americans, Hispanic Americans, Asian Americans and even white Americans. America itself has been enriched and improved by this energetic and dynamic movement.

Unfortunately, there have also been groups like the Black Panthers, the Nation of Islam and other such negatively oriented African American organizations that have fanned the flames of hatred and bigotry in the other direction. These groups encourage black separatism and chauvinism, and these in turn fuel more white bigotry.

Some white groups such as the Ku Klux Klan and the White Aryan Nation have used the black separatist groups as justification for their own calls for separating the races. They see the black organizations as vindicating their own existence. In fact they are very similar. Hate is the basis for all of them.

African Americans certainly have reason to view white-run America with healthy skepticism, and that doesn't make them militant racists. By the same token, very few white Americans are Ku Klux Klan material, but that does not mean they harbor no prejudicial attitudes.

A few minutes on Facebook will expose many racist whites, who would never dream of joining the KKK. In fact, they will tell you they are not racist. They are just telling you what they see in their daily lives. They will tell you there is never a riot, when a white suspect is killed by police. And they will tell that old story of the welfare queen buying steaks with food stamps, while talking on her smart phone, and then driving away in a Cadillac.

Many whites believe blacks are not always reasonable in their expectations. Furthermore, whites may not believe blacks are demanding enough of themselves as individuals or as a community. Many whites feel blacks are content to accept welfare or undemanding jobs rather than challenge themselves to excel.

Whites feel blacks are more tolerant of criminals in their communities. Where do these images originate? Experts say all stereotypes originate in truth. The falsehood is that they pertain to everyone in the group, not just the few who give rise to them.

An examination of the so called black community in America from a reasoned white perspective reveals a segment of society not unlike any other in general terms. There are leaders who contribute to their communities, their professions and to society as a whole. There are good family structures and broken ones, just as there are among other groups.

Most black families take pride in their homes and their neighborhoods. They are ambitious and want to achieve the same success that their white counterparts seek. They want an education for their children, good jobs, good medical care and fair treatment.

In short, they simply want to be sure they are judged and treated according to their personal merits, not their color.

However, every group has members who are not contributors to a positive image. Statistics reveal an obvious deterioration in the family make-up in the black community. Too many households are headed by single female parents. Yes, there are white families with the same problem, but not to the extent that is evident today in the black community.

The absence of so many fathers from the family environment adds to the instability felt by black children already depressed by lower economic means. Young black males especially are deprived of positive adult male role models.

Criminal elements flashing easy money through dealing drugs, prostitution, theft or other illegal means provide the missing role models to the detriment of these impressionable young people, thus leading a generation away from productive lives. If they also become parents, they will have no background for becoming responsible role models for their own children, and will foster another generation to perpetuate the cycle.

And what of the criminal element in black society. They are no worse than those among other ethnic or racial groups, but they seem to be more tolerated. If a white politician is caught dealing in drugs, the rest of the community wants him out of office and in jail.

But, the people of Washington, D.C. elected the late Marion Barry to city council as soon as he was out of jail. This puzzles whites, who feel African Americans are gullible when one of their own paints himself as a victim, when he is really a crook.

All a black criminal has to do is portray himself as a victim of white society, and the black community seems ready to overlook his criminal activities, even those that victimize other blacks, and welcome him back into the fold, even rewarding him in the process.

Had Rodney King been white, white Americans would have reacted much differently to his beating at the hands of the arresting officers. They might have criticized the officers for unnecessary brutality, but at the same time most would have felt King deserved some beating for his own actions, which even endangered lives during the high speed chase. He, himself, would have received little sympathy, even as the officers might have been criticized.

The thought of rioting over the verdict would be unthinkable in the white community, and, probably, in the Asian American community as well. African Americans saw white officers beating a black man. White Americans saw the police subduing a defiant and resistant law-breaker. The attitude of blacks is certainly molded by many generations of denial and discrimination.

African Americans feel if King had been white, the officers would not have beaten him. They identify with the situation of one who looks like them. Whites feel it is time to put aside such feelings and demand better conduct from everyone, white or black.

Of course, that is an easier assessment for whites. Most have never been the victims of such relentless bias. Sure, the Polish resent the Polish jokes. Yes, the Irish are angered at the image of the fight-prone drunk. The Germans don't like the jackboot image, and the Italians are not all mafiosi. But, by and large, these portrayals of various ethnic groups are merely annoying.

They are not constant, and they are not usually used to deny access to various institutions within our society. Even those foolish enough to believe such stereotyping of whole peoples seem not to discriminate against them on a regular basis. The stereotype images of blacks, however, have been and continue to be used to deny them the benefits of American society.

African Americans will have to become ever more demanding of members of their own community to overcome these prejudices. They will need to be completely intolerant of those among them who break criminal laws, and bring disgrace on the entire community. To be sure, the image of black America is in the hands of its own members to change.

It may not be right that every African American should bear the burden of correcting such stereotypes, but such stereotypes are steeped in reality somewhere, and there are times we are our brothers' keeper, even when he is heavy. Life is not fair.

It is not fair for Hispanic Americans, either. Some have a double whammy. They cannot speak English. They come from Puerto Rico, Mexico and South America. Some even come from Cuba. Some were born in the United States of immigrant parents, legal or illegal.

They are trapped in a system that holds out great wealth for them to see on television, in magazines and newspapers, but they seem unable as a group to attain most of what we call the American dream. They see it; they came here expecting it. But they can't get it.

Yes, some have done quite well. Some have risen to the highest levels of business, industry, the professions and even politics. Mayors, governors, members of Congress and even cabinet members can attest to that. But average Hispanic Americans are still behind, and racism seems to be the culprit.

What happened to the America they thought was awaiting them? They had always heard that America was the land where everyone was welcome; where everyone could find wealth and happiness; where everyone could be fulfilled. Where are all the good jobs? Where are the fine homes? Where is their chance?

They came to escape the poverty of their homelands and found poverty in America. Some feel they are treated worse than African Americans. They are treated as foreigners, as outsiders, despite the fact that many are from families born here for many generations.

They are denied the best jobs, sometimes because they are suspected of being illegal immigrants; many times because they cannot speak English well. They are treated with disdain by many whites. In fact, where there are large Hispanic communities, they are subjected to the same attitudes from whites that African Americans endure.

Whites, on the other hand, tend to feel that Hispanics are too lazy or lack the intelligence to learn the English language. This also adds to the difficulty Hispanics have in finding substantial employment. Many Hispanics have entered the professions and are as intelligent and competent as anyone else in our society, when given the education and opportunity to succeed.

But, unfortunately, there are countless numbers that seem to have given up trying to make it in America. White Americans are extremely intolerant of deviation from what they perceive is the norm. They don't understand people who come to America for what America offers and then retain their old customs, traditions, language and even dress.

In other words, if you're going to be American, be American. Learn the language and speak it. Learn the customs and adopt them. Dress American; look American; act American. Most Americans tend to feel threatened by an increasing population of non-English speaking residents. They hear the demand for government forms, even ballots, in other languages, and they fear the breakup of the American essence.

Language is the one common bond of a nation in the mind of most Americans. Look at the tension in Canada. Will Quebec ultimately secede? And what of Cyprus? One could just as easily point to Belgium or Switzerland, where various language groups appear to function quite well nationally.

But Americans, especially white Americans, fear that diverse official languages could lead eventually to the breakup of our national identity and the provincialization of America.

This might be the best point to recall the designation of English as our national language. The Continental Congress dealt with the issue long before we had a Constitution. There was an actual vote, and English won by one vote. Otherwise, we might all be speaking German.

But even at that, northern Vermont, Maine, New Hampshire and even part of New York have always had a sizeable number of native French speakers. After all, Quebec is right across the border. And when New Mexico came into the Union, the majority there spoke Spanish. So, let's not act as if those languages have no history here.

As with African Americans, Hispanic Americans, in order to increase acceptance among whites, must adopt a greater intolerance for criminal activity among their own. There is entirely too much criticism toward their members who act "too white". In both communities there is derision of those who excel or succeed by using the dominant culture and acclimating themselves to it.

Members of the Hispanic community should follow the leadership of those who are succeeding in America today. Instead, too many apparently are content to chastise the seeming abandonment of cultural precedent for material gain. They see this as cultural treason. One does not have to give up traditions or even a native tongue to add new ones.

Millions of immigrants to our shores over the last two hundred years managed to learn the English language and adopt the overall culture of American society without necessarily giving up their native ways or languages.

Asian Americans may be among the best examples of this. Most Asian immigrants over the years have been very conscientious in their drive to assimilate American culture. This was not out of disrespect for their homelands or their various traditions and languages.

On the contrary, their growth in the ways of this new land was a credit to their heritage. Asian Americans have always encouraged their children to excel in education and the pursuit of their goals. Most white Americans have great admiration for Asian Americans.

They seem to thrive on challenge. Of course, this is bigotry too, but it is positive bigotry.

Like many earlier immigrant groups, Asian Americans impress others with their willingness to work long hours for meager rewards at first in order to build their businesses and their communities. Such endurance cannot help drawing praise from anyone who witnesses it.

Usually, these people learn English and business customs quickly, and, within a generation, they have been accepted by almost all as natives. Only their appearance discloses their heritage.

This is not to suggest that they have given up the customs or language of their ancient homelands, or even that they are ashamed of their roots. Many maintain observance of cultural traditions at home, and some even continue to speak their former native tongue as a second language.

Whites don't seem to resent Asian Americans as a group to the extent that they do other ethnic or racial groups. There are certainly some fanatical bunches such as the Ku Klux Klan, who tend to hate anyone who is not a white anglo-saxon protestant, but these organizations are few, and their membership is not great.

Those who dislike Asian Americans fall largely into specific segments of society. Some die-hard World War II era patriots still consider the Japanese (and Japanese Americans) to be the "evil culprits" who started it all at Pearl Harbor. And there are veterans of Korea and Vietnam fighting who still bear a grudge against Koreans and Vietnamese.

There are a number of American workers who resent the competition from Asian labor markets and hold that competition and what they see as loss of American jobs against any Asian, including Asian Americans.

The Trans Pacific Partnership, like NAFTA, has brought renewed free trade hatred, because of the expected loss of American jobs, however, proponents argue there will be job increases. We shall see. And competition from China has brought renewed calls for trade barriers. But, Asian Americans as a group do not draw the kind of bigotry incurred by African Americans and Hispanic Americans.

Bigotry against Native Americans is largely a matter of regional import. There are parts of the United States where they are not noticed and, therefore, draw no rejection. In those areas where there are reservations, local white populations treat them much as blacks are treated in urban centers.

Most whites understand that the white man stole this land from the Indians, as many of them hate to be called, because it is in fact a misnomer, deriving from Columbus' error in thinking he had arrived in India.

The truth of the matter is that the white man stole nothing from the natives found in the new world. They owned nothing. They thought of themselves not as possessors of the land but as a part of it. What whites took from the Native American was the freedom to live off the land, the freedom to use the land and its animals and vegetation, the freedom to go and be where he would. Whites took freedom from the natives and imprisoned many on reservations, denying them the only way of existence they knew.

Today the Native Americans living on reservations and many living among the whites hate the whites for what they have lost and what they cannot now have. They have lower living standards, less access to education and business and job opportunities and higher unemployment and poverty levels than almost any ethnic group in America.

Alcoholism and fetal alcohol syndrome are rampant among Native Americans. Many industries set up on reservations by whites have taken advantage of cheap labor, and, by bribing some tribal officials, given little back to the Native American community. Those who wish to leave the reservations must first obtain permission from the federal Bureau of Indian Affairs in many cases. They may fair better outside.

There are a number of agencies and centers that offer assistance to Native Americans living in urban areas away from reservations. Federal grants and other monies made available from various sources help settle some in new homes, offer employment or job-finding services, and sometimes food and medical assistance to those who need it.

There are still those who would ridicule Native Americans by calling them names such as "Tonto" or "chief" or by making fun of their ancient culture with taunts about wigwams or peace pipes. This happens most often in communities near reservations, but occasionally one will hear such insensitive remarks in other areas as well from those who use ethnicity as a weapon.

If there is legitimate criticism of Native Americans as a group, it must come principally in two areas; the reluctance of many to join the Twenty-first Century and oversensitivity to public image.

It has been evident for a long time that those Native Americans who leave the reservation, obtain an education and mingle in the American culture and society with all others achieve levels of accomplishment comparable to every other American ethnic group, including whites. Why, then, continue to live in substandard conditions and pretend to continue a way of life that was normal over a century ago.

Average Germans do not wear lederhosen on a daily basis. Englishmen don't wear wigs, nor do their women wear bustles. Native Americans do not need to wear leathers and feathers as we wend our way through the era of space and technology.

Many militant Native Americans moan the loss of their cultural traditions, and at the same time they criticize the images used by some commercial interests, namely professional sports teams, to promote the teams' public persona and marketing efforts.

The Cleveland Indians are considering changing their logo to assuage Native Americans who resent the old one, which they say perpetuates certain negative stereotypes. The Atlanta Braves are being pressured to give up their "Tomahawk chop" trademark cheer. The Washington Redskins are criticized for a name some Native Americans consider racist. And the Kansas City Chiefs receive the same blasts.

Such sensitivity to everything that seems to exploit such images is not going to better the lot of the average Native American. On the contrary, such complaints use valuable energy, time and resources that could be doing something productive to increase educational and business opportunities for Native American youth.

Most ethnic groups in America would welcome such hidden praise as acknowledgment of competitive prowess. No one will ever hear a Scandinavian America complain about the Minnesota Vikings or their logo. They are justifiably proud of that bearded fighter with the horned helmet. It's time to quit complaining, get off the reservation and get into the mainstream of American life.

Most whites in America today do not hate other ethnic groups. They simply see too much complaining among minorities, some admittedly justifiable, and not enough effort to overcome past discrimination and adversity.

Most whites acknowledge that everyone is at least a little prejudiced, if only in favor of his own group. What disturbs them most is that many African Americans, Hispanic Americans and other such ethnic segments of our society will not admit to their own prejudices against each other and against whites.

Many in these communities choose to live among others in their racial or ethnic group because they do not wish to live around whites. Bigotry knows no color, and anyone can be guilty of hatred over race, creed or national origin. It is unacceptable from anyone. Racism is an element in society that retards the best development of everyone. Because of bigotry, we all lose.

MALE AND FEMALE HE CREATED THEM

For this reason a man leaves his father and mother, and clings to his wife...

Genesis

The American family has undergone a change in the last century like no other in the history of the human race. Less that eighty years ago the family in America, just as its counterparts in other countries around the world, included what we now call the extended family; all relatives by blood or marriage.

Our grandparents, aunts, uncles, cousins, various in-laws and many others stayed in close communication and thought of all as a unit. Today, in America, we loosely define our families as those we live with in the same dwelling, that is, the immediate family. We may include a divorced parent (an ever growing number today), but not always.

What has brought the American family to such a state, one that is unknown in most countries of the world, including our closely related European allies? What are the factors that have changed our attitudes on family? What influence have the Feminist and Gay Rights issues had? What can we do about the resulting problems, such as abortion, child abuse and child support enforcement? The view from the bottom is one of frustration at the enormity of these problems and the seeming insurmountability of the obstacles to solution. Still, some solutions come to mind, and even more questions come into better focus.

Human beings tend to divide everything into categories, including themselves. Racism is one of the many divisions that are used in a negative manner. Americans are like all others in that each would like to think he is separated from others by his better attributes. That then implies lesser characteristics in those he sees as less than himself or his group.

Separating groups according to race, color or nationality is not rational because it is based on accident of place or family of birth. These determinations are based more on who our parents were instead of who we are. It would seem more acceptable to judge another on that person's own choices and personal actions.

To some degree, various groups of Americans separate themselves from the mainstream, or at least what a great many like to believe is the mainstream. A large number of homosexuals in America would separate themselves from the heterosexual community. Many feminists seem to want a separation from men. Divorce has separated not only spouses from each other, but, to the detriment of our entire society, it has also deprived children of maturing with the help and guidance of both parents.

The abortion issue is typical of those issues which are so emotional, they tend to separate the extreme sides from all others as well as themselves from each other. We even separate older Americans from their own families in some ways; i.e. AARP, nursing homes, "retirement communities", etc. We are a nation of pidgeon-holers.

We like everything and everyone slotted neatly in a recognizable and convenient category. The average American will even give a self-describing label when asked in a given context. Each of us, if asked, will want to be considered liberal or conservative, blue collar or white, gay or straight, male or female, and any number of other labels we as Americans find so efficient for insulating ourselves from those we find inferior to ourselves. This is not to say these descriptions are incorrect, since many times they are quite accurate in as much as they ascribe a certain characteristic to oneself.

Nevertheless, some of these attempts to segregate social groups from each other have hurt American society in ways many of which may not even be known yet. The family, the neighborhood, the community and even the nation no longer seem as cohesive as they were even a few decades ago in this country.

These are the very institutions we must rely on for social stability and, ultimately, for our national security. How have we become who we are today? What has brought on the deterioration of the very foundation of our social makeup? What are the current forces affecting American social structure? Which divisions are beneficial, and which are not?

One of the most influential events in modern history insofar as affects us as a people was the Great Depression. A whole generation of Americans suffered through this catastrophic collapse of the economy of not only this country, but of the whole world. Unemployment reached almost thirty percent in the United States.

Families lost homes, possessions, savings, everything. Large businesses went bust. Banks failed. Depression described not only the economy, but the national spirit, our psyche, as well. And the government did nothing at first, thinking all would right itself eventually.

But people don't eat eventually; they eat everyday. Only those who lived through the Depression really understand the degree of suffering. It would affect the lives and the attitudes of all who survived it, and it would color their views and actions for life.

This was a generation that had little in childhood, and spent their youth on the battlefields and in the wartime factories of World War II. After so much hardship, they returned to post-war American society, ready to forge a future. They would have it better in adulthood than they did as children and young adults. They would find the good jobs of the booming post-war economy. They would build new communities and enlarge old ones. They would buy homes, spurring the homebuilding market, and they would buy cars, so many that the auto manufacturers became the barometer of the American economy for decades to come.

The fastest economic growth in American history produced the most affluent generation ever known anywhere on earth. They could be truly proud of the life they had built for their children. They were determined that their progeny would not suffer as they had. They would make sure their children had all the things they never had.

These children, the Baby Boomers as they would come to be called, became as a group the most affluent generation ever produced by any people in the history of the world. Within ten years they all had televisions. They could now be entertained instantly without leaving their homes. Along with this new medium came the TV dinner —- instant gratification of hunger, or even just desire.

Most had part time jobs or allowances, which gave them purchasing power. By the end of the decade of the fifties, many had automobiles, instant transportation. With all this the Baby Boomers were becoming ever more independent. They had all the things that any generation of children could want. Their parents had succeeded in making sure their kids had all the things they never had; that they would never suffer the pain of depression, and maybe they would even avoid war.

This was a generation of young who knew no serious want. On the contrary, television portrayed affluent families such as the Cleavers of Leave it to Beaver and the Andersons of Father Knows Best, where no problem was so serious, that it could not be solved in thirty minutes.

These were ideal families in which the father headed a household living comfortably on his ample income; the mother stayed home, cleaned her well appointed house, cooked and looked after the needs of her children, who were well-adjusted, well dressed and well off. These were the families we would all become, we thought.

And while we watched more and more television, we were bombarded by a barrage of the most sophisticated advertising ever launched anywhere. A captive audience with huge appetites for new conveniences and toys together with a comparatively large purse was now available to old and new businesses with an ever-expanding array of products and services.

Mobility, communication and monetary resources had created a generation with a gluttonous appetite for anything that might make life easier, more enjoyable or just more entertaining. Whole new industries were created to accommodate the tastes and whims of this fantastic new market.

The automobile after-market bulged with new products to decorate or care for all the cars now owned by teens and young adults, who took great pride in their new symbols of independence. Even songs were written about the cars; songs like Little Deuce Coupe, 409, and Hot Rod Lincoln.

The music recording industry changed its direction completely to take advantage of the most lucrative market ever available to it —-teenagers. The fashion industry aimed most of its advertising at the new clothing-conscious young purchasers, whose taste trends changed annually to the glee of designers. Not only was this the most affluent single generation in history, it was the largest.

This generation of Baby Boomers would dominate marketing strategies for the rest of the twentieth century, since they would become a larger and, hence, a more influential segment of the overall consumer market in America.

While the best description of the American economy was once "the business of America is business", the more appropriate paraphrase of that statement today is "the business of America is the Baby Boomers". They have been the first consideration in the vast majority of business decisions made in this country, especially those determining the direction of advertising.

Even now, with the Baby Boomers in their "prescription" years, drug stores abound on every corner. Retirement plans and vacation spots cater to a huge market. The new strains on the Social Security and Medicare funds are a major concern for our national budget, but we will address that elsewhere.

The demands of the Baby Boomers on the market place and on the whole of society in America are in all likelihood the major determinant of the direction in which the institutions of contemporary America are moving. It may be said that those who came out of the Depression and World War II set in motion through their children the forces that would create the American society that would define the rest of the twentieth century and carry us well into the twenty-first.

All that is good and certainly all that is bad in America today can be traced to that one overwhelming event —- the Great Depression. The we-generation that survived it gave birth to the me-generation; a generation that demands much, but gives little; a generation of enormous appetite for the best in life, but little sense of responsibility to the generation that gave so much to them or even to the generation that they themselves have produced. What has the Baby Boomer generation done for America? What has it brought or wrought for the generations that will follow?

The American Family

The Andersons and the Cleavers are gone now, not just from television, but even from the American dream. No one now hopes for such a family. We know now that it never really existed except in the make-believe world of electronic entertainment. We all wanted these families to be real. We wanted a world of quick solutions and harmony.

Most of us never had harmony in our lives such as was shown by these fantasies. We even knew it as we watched them. It was such a nice thought, however, that maybe some family somewhere

61

might actually experience such a worry-free, trouble-free daily life, that we held it up as a model of what our families would be when we grew up and set out on our own.

After all, if we could dispel boredom by turning on the TV for thirty minutes, if we could assuage a whim of appetite by popping a TV dinner into the oven, or now the microwave, for a few minutes or seconds, if we could overcome a moment of loneliness by jumping into a car and driving several miles to visit a friend, why could we not solve any real life problem facing any family in some equally simple fashion. Surely, our families would, indeed, resemble those of the Cleavers and the Andersons.

But, a different world faced this optimistic generation, since their optimism was based more on desire than on commitment. The decade of the 1950's is sometimes referred to as the age of innocence, an apt description for a decade which saw American youth absorbed in hot cars, sodas, dance crazes and self-indulgence.

Those children of means wanted for little; those of limited resources, or none, fantasized about a future when they would share the same "good life". No matter what their individual stations in life, they all saw a life in which every problem life could pose could be solved instantly. The demands and needs of a spouse and children were no different from other problems in life. No work or struggle would be necessary. There must be a simple solution to even the most complex difficulty.

By historical measures, the results of this simplistic view of life were instantaneous. The Baby Boomers reached adulthood with a loud thud. That was the sound of age-old institutions falling, as the Boomers discarded them one by one, when they proved too much trouble to maintain.

The family was the first to go. It never occurred to most of the Boomers, that marriage was a give and take arrangement; that each partner had to surrender, as it were, a bit of personal independence; that each would have to accommodate some of the eccentricities of the other. This was, after all, the spoiled generation that had come to expect instant gratification and instant satisfaction from all situations and from all people. Each spouse in many cases expected all accommodation to come from the other.

The solution to friction between spouses, and sometimes to the normal demands of family life, was not compromise, not commitment, not joint efforts of family members, but divorce.

Divorce rates skyrocketed among Baby Boomer marriages, when compared to any previous generation. Of course, there were a great many marriages that survived and prospered, but more than ever before marriages were breaking up, and families were failing. The new attitude seemed to be one of intolerance of any circumstance that seemed to be too demanding, too stressful or just too inconvenient.

We were a generation of throwaway paper plates and paper cups, of throwaway car parts, of throw away TV's. Why not throw away an uncomfortable marriage, much like an uncomfortable shirt, and simply get a new one?

CHILD SUPPORT ENFORCEMENT

This naturally works much better if there are no children involved. More often than not, however, it seems there were children. What happens to the children of such a marriage? They are the forgotten ones.

They usually end up with their mother, living in poverty or close to it. Many require public assistance for basic needs, including medical care. The number of deadbeat dads in this country today is a national disgrace. These children grow up without the beneficial influence of half of their parents.

They are commonly undernourished and under-nurtured. They develop more slowly, achieve less as a group, and generally add to a growing underclass in American society. As a result of the deterioration of the American family, we have a growing number of unstable and unproductive individuals in society.

This destabilizes society itself, lowering productivity, eroding our national competitiveness in the world, and ultimately weakening us as a nation.

Add to this the general feeling of resentment among the taxpayers who must bear the burden of supporting these children and their mothers. This resentment is expressed in the tendency to vote against new taxes for infrastructural improvements, for schools or just the cost of running local government.

The attitude of the voters is not good in this country due to many factors, but this anger at having to tax ourselves to support children who have living parents is a principal cause of voter disenchantment with the system. Hence, the support President Clinton received during the 1992 election due to his emphasis on overhauling the welfare system, in particular, child support enforcement.

The next two administrations swayed back and forth on this issue, as did the public. Conservatives seem to tire of helping the poor altogether, while liberals demand more and more help.

But, then, every politician who seeks an office associated even remotely with support enforcement promises to "get tough" with deadbeat dads. After two decades of such promises, the public is justifiably skeptical of any candidate offering such assurances. The campaign rhetoric is always stronger than the commitment to follow through.

Moreover, the courts are notoriously lenient with these culprits, while at the same time claiming to be strict with those who violate court mandated support. Most judges assert that there is no place to put the violators.

Jails are already crowded with populations bulging with more dangerous types. Taxpayers are not ready to pay the price of more and bigger prisons. So what should we do with absent parents under order to support their own children?

Some are unemployed and claim they are unable to make the money necessary to comply with court orders for support. Some are underemployed and say they are living hand to mouth themselves. Still others are remarried and have new families and children to support, and they would be forced to take from their second (or third, or…) set of children to meet such legal obligations.

Maybe we should try to look at this problem from the point of view of the neglected children. They did not cause the problems that separated their parents. They cannot fend for themselves. They need care. They need a chance to develop in an atmosphere as worry free as possible. Why should a child have to support himself?

Since society stands to lose if any child, let alone so many, grows to adulthood requiring continued public support, it is for society to ensure that every child has the optimum chance to grow and find success within that society. This not only assures that individual child an opportunity to achieve all that heredity and environment together can offer, but it further provides an even better chance for the generation that follows.

The American welfare system is on the verge of collapse under the weight of the demands of those who should be cared for by persons with the natural obligation to do so. Every society must help those members whose circumstances leave them unable to attend to their own needs, but those capable of caring for themselves and their offspring must be required to do so.

The question remains, "How do we enforce that requirement?" Many under court orders to support their children will honor that obligation only insofar as the consequences of disobeying the order force them to comply. That is, unless the punishment for noncompliance is severe and certain, many will ignore the orders.

Love of their own children seems insufficient motivation to move them to adhere to their obligations. Therefore, society must institute whatever means are necessary to ensure that they follow the orders of proper authority. Perhaps, there might be created a system of farms operated with the labor provided by the parents who for whatever reason fail to provide the necessary support.

Those who claim unemployment or underemployment would then have a way to meet their obligations. Those who are remarried or have other situations that seem to take all their available resources might then have the motivation to "find" more adequate income to satisfy their responsibilities.

Income surplus from the farms would provide for the children of those who worked the farm. In this way honest labor would provide honorable income for those who most deserve it, the children.

What of the freedom of the violators? What about their constitutional rights? How can we in America establish such a system in apparent violation of our own constitution? There is nothing the U.S, Constitution that allows the abandonment of children, that grants a "right" to create children wantonly without true intent to care for them, that denies children the right to grow and learn and mature with the support of the parents who bore them.

Since when does the Constitution deny the majority the right to the fruits of their labor through taxation in order to allow some privileged few to escape their own moral as well as legal obligation to sustain the children they parented?

No, freedom in America cannot be freedom from responsibility for the results of our own actions. We must instill in each person in our culture that a parent must be held accountable for raising his or her own children, to include the financial responsibility no matter what the parent's means. To do less is not only the unconscionable abandonment of our children, but, as a society, an unreasonable endorsement of blatant antisocial behavior.

Children, however, are not the only members of contemporary American society that seem neglected by the Baby Boomer generation. Let us not forget the generation that created this Frankenstein.

Having produced this strange social anomaly, the parents of many Boomers now find themselves in need of care, be it financial, medical or, perhaps just TLC, and where are their logical caretakers? Their children, more than any generation in modern history, are seemingly inclined to forsake them and leave their fate to the general public. Previous generations of young adults would have found such an attitude morally repugnant.

Whatever happened to "honor thy father and thy mother"? This is not just biblical, it is essential to orderly transition and growth in any society. The bonds between any two generations determine the strength of the bonds that hold society itself together, for, if we feel no attachment to our parents or to our children, then how can we sustain the bonds that hold us together as a community or as a nation?

And if there be no loyalty to family, can there exist any great loyalty to country or even to the ideals and truths we hold dear as a people?

What kind of society or group within a society so easily relegates its elderly to nursing homes, when many could live quite well at home with assistance of family? Why do so many elderly in America live in so-called "retirement communities", separated from their families?

What kind of government can allow many who are retired to lose everything they have spent a lifetime building to a catastrophic illness? Many in this latter group have been forced to divorce a spouse to avoid financial devastation in order to qualify for help from public sources.

This is not acceptable in the America founded by visionaries and built by pioneers who were sustained in the face of unimaginable adversity by love, family and a belief in a land of opportunity for all.

We must cope as a nation with the disintegration of the family as
we once knew it, and the manifestations thereof in today's
American society. If we do not resolve the negative impact on us,
we will incur even further damage to our most vulnerable
members, our children and our elderly.

CHILD ABUSE

The stress of family life in the last decade of the twentieth century,
together with this loss of close family relationships has brought a
rise in physical abuse among family members, particularly abuse
of parents and children.

New laws are cropping up in a number of states to deal with abuse
of the elderly, and there have always been some laws regarding
child abuse, but still it persists. This is especially true, it appears, in
broken or dysfunctional families.

The number of children suffering severe injuries and even death at
the hands of their parents or of some person living with a parent is
not just alarming; it is a cry for help from those who need our help
most. We cannot fail. We dare not.

It is most obvious that our current laws are not sufficiently punitive
or corrective to deter this appalling crime against the weak and
innocent. What kind of society can permit the brutal, cowardly and
merciless beating of a child?

Babies only days old have been brought to hospitals to die of
internal injuries from assaults from the fists of grown men. We
have monsters among us. The prophet Jeremiah said, "in those
days they will kill their own children." That could easily describe
these times.

Children have always been subject to parental discipline, and
sometimes that discipline has taken the form of corporal
punishment, but it was administered with love. Many a child has
heard the proverbial, "This will hurt me more than you." There
was a time when we could be sure this was true.

Today, young parents who are ill-prepared for life, much less parenthood, are thrust into the problems that come with having children. They have problems with carrying out their responsibilities in the financial world, holding a job, maintaining a household, and attending to the needs that come with marriage.

Then they have children, often before they are ready for the new demands of parenting. Sometimes they begin to blame the child(ren) for the financial burden they have increased, or for the new stresses between the parents, or between the parent and friend (today's arrangement).

Maybe it is the unrelated lover of the parent who finds the child an intrusion into the relationship with the parent. Then there are the times when the child just happens to be in the wrong place at the wrong time. The unstable adult just grabs the first person available on whom he can inflict his rage at society.

Whatever the reason or cause, we as a people cannot tolerate those who are so unstable and unable to deal with life that they torture and kill our young to express their immature frustrations with life. We have to send a clear signal that this country, this nation, this people will not accept such behavior and will not allow such monsters to dwell among us.

Punishment must be severe and swift and sure. No penalty is too severe for any adult who would beat a child to death. What is beyond belief is that in our current penal codes is provision for parole and/or probation for such offenders. There are many documented cases in which a convicted child beater or killer commits the same offense while on parole or probation for an earlier infraction. This problem is more a result of the lack of enforcement of penalties in our penal system and will be discussed in a later section.

Our first order of business in this area is to strengthen and stiffen the penalties for child abuse. Naturally, every effort must be made to verify accusations made by children, who may make false or exaggerated claims to retaliate against strict parents, or who may make charges at the behest of an estranged spouse.

But once the rights of the accused have been safeguarded and a conviction obtained, the penalties must be sufficient to deter others who might allow themselves to be involved in such an act, and , if at all possible, they must insure that the offender will never be able to repeat such a despicable assault on a child.

ABORTION

This new awareness of child abuse and the emotional reaction to it that we as a nation have had accompanies what has become perhaps the most emotional dispute ever debated by the American public. There are very few Americans that have not formed an opinion on the issue of abortion and access to it. It is a volatile subject which evokes strong feelings from each individual according to that person's attitudes toward biology, religion, society and a host of other variables in human existence.

To the radicals at either end of the issue, it is a clear cut matter with no gray area. Unfortunately, that is not the case for the vast majority in between. There are, in fact, logical arguments both for and against easier access to abortion.

There have been times in American history when the practice was quite common and suffered no serious opposition from any quarter. To be sure, abortion has been accepted and denounced by our society alternately from one era to another. The greatest opposition has not always come from religious groups.

The medical community had opposed it at the turn of the last century, because midwives performed most of the procedures, thus denying control of the medical conditions and the fees to the medical professionals. One must make the mental decision which weighed most heavily on the minds of the physicians in spurring their opposition. Today, when the operations must be performed by a physician, the American Medical Association is decidedly Pro-Choice.

The best point to be made in defense of availability of abortion is the history of illegal abortion in America and the bloody record of botched procedures and the deaths or serious injury of so many young women, who out of desperation or for whatever reason felt compelled to seek the operation at the hands of unqualified or disqualified persons.

The argument is that, if a woman has decided she is going to have an abortion and kill her fetus, it should not be necessary for her to risk her own death as well. After all, her death will not save the fetus.

The lack of a legal determination of exactly when life begins also lends to the Pro-Choice defense that this act is not murder, since the fetus is not yet a human being. At the very least, it is debated, a woman should make the decision, because it is she, who must carry the child to term, at some risk to her own health, financial security and sometimes her personal reputation in the community.

In addition, she may not be in a position to rear a child, or of a nature to give up to adoption an infant she will always know is her own. The principle point on this side of the debate is that it is the constitutional right of any woman to make a decision regarding her own body without the interference of any person or institution, notwithstanding anyone else's opinion or belief regarding the way she executes that right.

The other side, of course, disagrees. In their minds, the rights of at least one person are being disregarded in the performance of every abortion…the child that is aborted. The constitution is supposed to protect the right of each person to life, liberty and the pursuit of happiness. The first of these is the right to life, and the Pro-Life faction feels that right starts at conception.

They have at least some logic in their side, in that the lack of a legal definition of when life begins leaves that issue open, and one can logically argue in favor of going all the way back as far as possible, to conception.

We know life does not start before conception and that it does start somewhere after it but before birth. Where do we draw the line? Why would it not be arbitrary to pick any particular point in fetal development and designate that as the beginning of life? Who will make that decision?

Furthermore, if the fetus is a living human being, does it not deserve the protection of the constitution? It is not an animal. Science assigns a species to every living thing on earth. By genetic makeup the fetus proves itself to be a human being.

Since every human being is arguably a person, it deserves the protection of the constitution. But the constitutional argument is not the principle issue to the radical Pro-Life movement. Their mainstay is the moral issue. Life is too precious to take in what they consider an act of convenience. They argue that the vast majority of abortions do not involve a threat to the life or health of the mother.

In these cases it is an act, therefore, of convenience for the mother, as she is merely trying to undo the consequences of an earlier act she may, in fact, already greatly regret. Since rape and incest account for only about four percent of the pregnancies that end in abortion, we must conclude that the other ninety-six percent involve voluntary sexual relations involving the subject woman.

Would it not be more socially and morally correct to abstain from conduct likely to result in unwanted pregnancy. Yes, some of those pregnancies resulted from acts between married partners, whose birth control method simply failed. This, however, involves but a small fraction and doesn't detract from the argument?

Most abortions are actually performed as a means of birth control. The woman does not want a child, but she was not careful enough. Now she wants to correct the error at the expense of another human being. This is the most abhorrent and unacceptable implication to the Pro-Lifers. This to them is an affront to our creator.

On the other hand, the Pro-Choice faction can make a legitimate religious argument in favor of their side. The Bible says that God gave humans the choice individually between good and evil. That is to say God gave everyone the right to sin.

Forget the rights protected by the Constitution. What right do we have as a society to take away a right granted to every person by God, himself….the right to sin. If we are "endowed by our creator with certain inalienable rights", even the pregnant woman has them.

On that basis, religious and moral authority can be easily construed, it seems, to support either radical extreme in this volatile debate. But, surely, there must be some middle ground, on which neither side agrees completely, but both acknowledge enough gain to accede to compromise. For now, each side is content to continue to criticize the other for its reprehensible conduct.

The Pro-Lifers have sit-ins and demonstrations inside and outside abortion clinics. Since they are doing "God's work", their actions are justifiable on their own moral grounds. They do, in fact, persuade some women to reconsider the act they are considering, but there are a great many who feel exploited over an issue over which they already have ambiguous feelings. Some radicals have even resorted to murdering a doctor over this issue. Nevertheless, the radicals on this side of the issue feel they are accomplishing something, if they can save just one baby from slaughter.

If it were not for their belligerence, they could stake out the high ground in this battle by simply pointing out who is quietly supporting the other side, namely, the doctors, the nurses and the clinic owners. They are not performing these procedures for the public good or out of a sense of charity.

They are in many cases making a fortune off the misfortune of women who are depressed over their plight and scared. While the Pro-Choicers hail these medical facilities and their operators as heroes for providing what they see as a much needed service, the

Pro-Lifers see them as ogres and parasites for sucking their affluence from a body of suffering humanity.

Surely, such hostile adversaries can find a way to lay down their social weapons and bring peace to a segment of our population that has known only strife and adversity. There is so much on which they could agree. The women in need are important to both. The unnecessary pregnancies are avoidable.

One could more easily accept the sincerity of either or both, if they were to show a willingness to meet on common ground to find solutions rather than recrimination. It may be that the leaders of each side are more concerned with their own notoriety than with the welfare of women in need and their threatened progeny. Though they both speak of their Creator and His wishes, they may face His wrath for their refusal to "love one another."

FEMINISM

The champion of abortion rights and the vanguard of women's rights in general in America today is the Feminist movement. Since the beginning there has been some form of women's rights activity, some organized, some not, in this country. That the founders of American democracy left women completely out of the process and the vote accounts for the principal direction of the early activists.

After they had won the vote, there seems to have been no focus for American women for several decades, but, following World War II, when many women remained in the work force, resentment began to grow against the discrimination in favor of male employees, who very often made more money than their female counterparts for the same work.

There was at first no effort even to disguise the bias. Employers made no secret of their feelings that these men are the principal support for their families, and, in the view of most Americans, working women were holding down jobs that some male breadwinners needed. Besides, they should be home making cakes and babies and taking care of their husbands and families.

If they had none, they should spend their time trying to land a man to give them a purpose in life. Women were treated as second class people. Husbands and boyfriends would beat their wives and companions with impunity, and most people felt "she must have asked for it" or "she should try not to provoke him." They were considered almost as chattel.

Abused wives who complained were commonly sent back to the abusing husband. Sometimes husbands were summoned to police stations to retrieve a runaway wife who was caught by the authorities.

If a woman were lucky enough and persistent enough to be granted a divorce, she was probably destitute. Few had skills to fill a decent, well paid position. They usually had the children and received little or no support from the former spouse. Most stayed in the abusive relationship for the good of the children or because of intimidation, physical and financial.

Then came the sixties, the decade of turmoil. The Baby Boomers were changing all the other social mores, and the time was ripe for another women's rights movement to accompany the civil rights movement. The Women's Liberation Movement, as it was then called, demanded equality with men, in the work place, in the family and throughout society.

There were demonstrations. The radicals in the movement burned their bras in defiance of the male sexist attitude toward women. One thing differentiated them from the earlier suffrage movement. This time they already had the vote, and, as they were half the population, this was the most powerful weapon they could have. The politicians began listening intently to their demands. Laws were passed to bar discrimination in the work place based on gender. Equal work would now mean equal pay.

Also, women began to rebel against sexual harassment. They were tired of being groped, pinched and teased as females. They no longer countenanced innuendo regarding their sexuality. They especially refused to tolerate hints that their success at work depended on the sexual favors they might provide to their superiors.

They demanded and got new laws regarding divorce and child support. They were part of the Baby Boomer generation that know no tolerance for inconvenience, discomfort or, most especially, abuse.

But the pendulum swings both ways, and sometimes from one extreme to the other. Where women once were treated as if they had little value and no rights, now they would demand to be treated as if they were men. That is not to say "equal" to men, but "same" as men. There is a great difference. Men and women are certainly equal in their general abilities, intelligence and as human beings, but they are not the same.

Men will never bear children, and they generally don't have the same tolerance for discomfort that women have. On the other hand, women cannot on average perform the kind of heavy physical labor that men can. In all of nature there is usually a division of labor, some to males, some to females. Why should humans be different?

This is not to suggest that there is no overlap of abilities. There are relatively few tasks that only one gender can do well, so there is no logic to excluding anyone from most jobs on the basis of gender. There still exists good reason for women to resent the discrimination that takes place in many work situations today.

There are still male chauvinists who cannot adjust to a world of equal opportunity and equal access without sexual liaisons or innuendo. There remains substantial room for improvement either through new laws or enforcement of existing law. And an additional problem has come to the fore. Many men are rebelling against a movement they see taking some of what they consider their jobs, and they feel intimidated by newly empowered women.

On the criminal level, the number of rapes and other assaults on women has increased dramatically during the past several decades, although there is a legitimate claim that the rate is much the same, but reporting is more frequent and more accurate.

Much of the increase is attributed to the perceived threat of liberated women in a society once dominated by males, many of whom now feel somewhat emasculated by the strong American woman.

This violence against women is seen at all levels of society, although it is more prevalent at lower economic strata. Men seem especially unable to cope with female aggressiveness in two previously male-dominated preserves —- the bedroom and the boardroom.

It might be added that even the Congress has had an influx of women. Both houses now have significant groups of women; such will affect national attitudes and laws in every area. After several attempts to elect national tickets that included women, there is a very good chance we will elect a woman President in the very near future.

Women today experience a new found freedom to initiate sexual encounters, and they are quite comfortable controlling complex business situations. In either circumstance, they seem to have attained a new confidence in advancing their own leadership.

Some male egos cannot withstand such a turnaround in control. But there is more. There is also a growing resentment of men and even some women to the militancy exhibited by many in leadership roles in the Feminist movement. Some have clearly gone too far.

Men and women are different; equal, but different. The worst characteristic of the movement is that it tries to obscure or even deny this biological fact. The extremes to which the Feminists will go to emphasize their "sameness" with men seemingly have no bounds. Even our language is fair game.

That language is an expression of a culture in its forms, construction and vocabulary would appear to make it a reasonable target for alteration in the face of movement against all forms of discrimination.

Language, after all, is a means of discrimination and a repository for terms of bias. Obviously, there was a time when all firemen, policemen and foremen were men. Firefighters and police officers include women, and the terms are not uncomfortable. But "forewoman" tastes foreign. Chairwoman is now acceptable, but it is still awkward, though not as awkward as chair, which is still a piece of furniture.

Feminists are intent on rooting out such terms in the English language. Thus, the term Ms. was made up to replace the offensive (to some) Miss. There was a strong feeling against any term that carried with it the marital status of women, who resent any attempt to describe any woman by her marital situation.

But, why have American Feminists, apparently alone among world feminists, sought to change their language to accommodate this social movement. Other languages have gone almost untouched by such controversy.

The Spanish term for an unmarried woman is Senorita, which by derivation from its Latin source means "little old woman". Even the married woman, Senora, is an "old woman". The Italian Signorina and Signora have the exact same meanings. The French Madame is "my lady" and Mademoiselle is "my little lady". These are almost as patronizing.

The English "sir" is derived from the French Sieur (lord) which itself comes from Seignieur which in turn comes from the Latin for "old man". Yet, men don't complain. It would seem silly to men to take offense at what a word used to mean. Men are only concerned with now.

Speaking of now, no discussion of Feminism in American would be complete without a mention of the National Organization for Women (NOW). Formed originally as a support group for women's rights advocates, it has unfortunately degenerated into a body most American women don't regard with confidence as their representative in this public discussion.

NOW is today more concerned with the lot of gays and lesbians, abortion seekers, AIDS prevention and cure and a host of fringe issues, than in the problems of working women and women who choose to stay home in a traditional role. It almost denigrates the role of housewife and mother, since few of these are marching for those fringe causes.

It could now be more accurately described as the National Organization for Militant Feminists. It is unfortunate in light of the great hope it evoked at its birth as a leader for women's issues.

GAY RIGHTS

The Gay Rights Movement does not need NOW to espouse its cause. It has become in recent years a loud voice in pursuit of equal status for the lifestyle of gays and lesbians in the United States. Growing from a relatively quiet existence in "the closet" just a few years ago, it, too, has become increasingly militant in the pursuit of its goals.

Gays and lesbians have taken a higher profile in the business world, the entertainment industry and, of course, politics. As with the other civil rights causes, the sixties proved to be a watershed decade for this movement. But now, the new millennium has sparked the forefront of the movement, with the majority of Americans now favoring equal treatment under the law for lesbians, gays, bisexuals and trans-genders.

There is no question that the gay lifestyle has been around for a long time. It has existed throughout history. In most cultures it has been regarded as an aberration, and gays have been persecuted and sometimes killed by intolerant contemporaries in countless cultures throughout the ages.

Even among confessed bigots, other minority groups are not nearly as distasteful as gays. And this despite the lack of violence of gays toward heterosexuals. Most homosexual men and women appear to be very sensitive and caring. They have an image that conjures up such descriptive words as gentle, soft, helpful, tender, artful and creative. And, yet, most of the "straight" community resents and resists them.

They are often not welcome in schools, churches, businesses or any of the centers of social exchange in the average American community. The unacceptability of their lifestyle makes it difficult if not impossible for the average heterosexual to interact with them in any context.

Their sexual preference is considered abnormal, and the attitude toward them from others ranges from tolerance to disdain, even though evidence of late indicates that their sexual preference is genetic in origin.

The general public is not of one mind on this issue, however, many would not want to live around openly homosexual people. There is still the lingering suspicion that, despite the consensus reached two decades ago that homosexuality is not a dysfunction but a genetic disorder, it is a chosen lifestyle.

The American Psychiatric Association labelled homosexuality a disorder after almost a century of attempts to treat gays and cure or rehabilitate them. After so many failures and so many studies, it was decided the aberrant behavior was not a result of maladjustments in life, but was instead a function of genetic determinants.

Many segments of our societal structure have accepted this view over the years, but there still remains a significant number who refuse to believe that gays and lesbians cannot learn conventional sexual behavior and preference.

This simply intensifies the feelings of the general public that gays and lesbians, as well as bisexuals and trans-gender individuals, if they insist on living in that lifestyle, should maintain their privacy to the degree that they keep their activities in the closet, so to speak.

That includes gays in the military. Those who have not served in the military do not understand how disturbing the open presence of gays and lesbians would be to the good order and discipline that is necessary to the proper functioning of our defense establishment. Still, since allowing gays in the military, they have proven as effective as others and not disruptive at all.

Even though the issue has been settled, and gays now served openly, there are some who cannot countenance the mixture of gays and straights in military units. The issue goes beyond privacy in the shower and in sleeping quarters. A reduced level of respect is present among some heterosexuals for their gay counterparts.

Military personnel must function as a unit in combat and in many other military situations. Lack of confidence in any single member can destroy the effectiveness of the entire unit. But now that the policy has been changed for a time, the negatives that were expected have gone largely unrealized. Military commanders have said they saw no change in readiness or effectiveness.

Some would compare this expected problem of effectiveness damaged by the presence of unwanted members to the integration of African American members into the armed services in the late 1940's, and the reality matches the earlier expectation based on race. When will we ever have the character to say we were wrong?

Gays and lesbians have served in the U.S. military services with honor and continue to do so, but it can be argued that one of the reasons for their oft times exemplary service has been that their sexual preference was kept secret. Had the facts been general knowledge, it can be said, they might not have had the opportunity to prove their abilities and their bravery. Their competence would have been overshadowed by the recognition of their "condition" by their comrades. How unfortunate!

The subsequent rejection and ultimate discharge would have prevented them from achieving their military successes. What a loss for our country! The question on the military applications regarding sexual preference has been eliminated. Under these conditions, a gay or lesbian who wishes to serve in any military service and who can meet the demands of military life, can serve with honor.

Despite the fact that homosexuality is so offensive to some average heterosexual Americans and the lifestyle of the gay and lesbian community is considered so distasteful, there can be no excuse for those who would physically abuse or in any way do harm to a gay or lesbian simply because of a disgust for that lifestyle.

Every human being is entitled to live in peace while meeting civic obligations to respect others, and everyone has the same entitlement to the kindness of others. In other words, laws should acknowledge and protect the rights of every American, regardless of any attribute which may be unique to a particular person.

Now that same sex marriage has been ruled legal and legitimate throughout the nation, there is a general public acceptance almost everywhere. There are pockets of dissent and even resistance, but in time most people will accept the rights of everyone to live as they choose. It's American.

If the family that is the human race is to survive, we must all see each other as family, even those who like some family members will do exhibit behavior we find abnormal or just unacceptable.

The Baby Boomer generation has varied and complicated our society so much as to make us complete strangers as a society to our ancestors of only two generations ago. Some of the changes are good and should be accepted gleefully; others are detrimental, and reversal should be attempted for the sake of our children and future generations to come.

Rebellion is the byword of this generation. Stability and civility must become the mark of those who followed this generation.

We have discarded many of the values of all past generations of Americans. What we have instituted in their place is of questionable worth. We are paying a price for these wholesale modifications made with such cavalier nonchalance. May the judgment of our grandchildren be kind.

EDUCATION

Human history becomes more and more a race between education and catastrophe.

H. G. Wells

What the United States is and what it becomes is directly related to the education that prepares our children for life and for citizenship. For years, nay decades, those at the top have "addressed" the deterioration of the system by which we educate our children in America. It seems a constant parade of social problems draws more and more of our attention, and that of our teachers, away from the elements of education that are required in the complex society and world we face today.

Instead of focusing on mathematics, reading, science and the other basic tools of success, the teachers of today must attend first to stresses arising from broken families, lack of parental guidance or care, gang activities, drug abuse or sales, pregnancy, communicable diseases and a myriad of other non-education related topics. How did we let this happen? Only a couple generations ago we had the premier education system in the world.

The education of the Baby Boomers was the finest provided by any country anywhere. When did it change? Why did it change? What changed? What should we do to fix the problem? What can we do? In order to answer these questions, we must first look at what we had, how it evolved, and what forces were at work in American society during the past fifty years or so.

First, where did the schools that brought a generation of Americans into the Space Age, the consumer age, the age of modern convenience go? After World War II, the new post-war families settled into their jobs and their homes, and proceeded to raise children.

Dad went to work, mom stayed home to take care of the home and the little ones, and the school-aged children went off to learn readin', writin' and 'rithmetic. They also got a good dose of advanced math and science courses, thanks to the strong emphasis on America's new role as leader of the free, non-communist world.

We had a crucial need to ensure that we had a citizenry educated enough to provide the leadership in industry, research and government, that we knew we would need to maintain our pre-eminent position vis-a-vis the potential aggressors in the Soviet empire.

So urgent was this need for academic excellence, that we not only beefed up our public school curriculum, we even encouraged all students to consider seeking higher education at the college level. To make this easier the U.S. government provided loans with extremely low interest rates and deferred interest and payment schedules to promote the availability of a college education to everyone, regardless of financial means.

America was serious about building a populace more educated than any in history. Schools were given previously unheard of levels of funding. Voters passed issue after issue to improve facilities and salaries. Teachers' salaries became comparable with those of other professions, so much so that a large influx of new teachers was attracted to the system.

New subjects in the post war curriculum brought not only newly trained teaching personnel, but government and industry grants as well. Demand from these new consumers strained the supply, and the schools thrived in their new found prominence in American society.

We, who were students in that positive atmosphere, benefitted immensely from the accent on success and from the attitudes of the teachers, the administrators and even our parents. They all seemed to work in harmony with their only goal being our successful attainment of that most beneficial and productive societal tool —- an education.

Yes, there were problems at times keeping up with the pace and meeting objectives, but by and large we were happy in school. We learned in class; we learned at athletic events; we learned at dances and at parties. We learned. And we graduated in record numbers.

Some went to work. Some went on to further education. We became what our parents intended —- the most educated and the most prepared generation in the history of this nation or any other. But, something happened to America along the way.

Somewhere we lost our focus. Or, maybe we just failed to keep up with the ever changing demands of an increasingly complex century. Whatever the cause, our society continued to grow and to develop, but our schools did not. Socially, they did, but academically and operationally they did not.

Children came to school with new problems, but the system had only the old solutions, solutions which were not adaptable to satisfy the needs of the generation preparing for the twenty-first century.

Since all education begins in the home, we must look at the changes in the family as an institution in order to assess properly the changes that followed in the schools. As noted in the discussion on the post World War II generation known as the Baby Boomers, our whole society changed as this generation went through their childhood and matured to become today's parents.

The previous generation of parents had been somewhat selfless and traditional. They were patient, caring, sacrificing and generous with their children; so much so that the children grew to expect and even demand immediate gratification of every whim. This was the generation of instant solutions to even the most insignificant problems.

Spouses who became problems were discarded. Often, children, who are all problems until we raise them, are discarded as well. These children now lived in one-parent homes, where the one parent is either holding down a job and struggling to be a parent at home at the same time, or that parent is on public assistance, barely making ends meet and feeling like a failure as a parent for not having the means to provide all of what the children need.

The absent parent often shows no concern for the children and does little to support or guide them. Thus, the two parents nature intended are denied to those too young to learn alone.

Why do we need both parents? Some don't, but one theory says that mothers treat children like children always; fathers demand that they grow up. This seems sensible.

One might suspect, therefore, that a single-parent family in which the mother is the parent would tend to raise dependent, immature children who remain childish and demanding, never quite able to graduate to a higher level of achievement. There are probably plenty of children in schools today from this type of home who could bear out this theory. They have no discipline at home and do not respond well to any at school.

The other single-parent family, the one with the single father, might tend to overemphasize discipline almost to the exclusion of tenderness. This would logically produce children who feel unloved and rebel against any authority out of anger and hurt. These children would seek attention, even negative attention, to replace the love they feel they are denied.

Of course, these are theoretical situations, and there are certainly some excellent single parents who are adept at providing the love and discipline their children need. It is just as likely, however, that this generation of parents is sending to school a great many children lacking the necessary emotional preparation and support to maximize their educational opportunities.

Some statistics indicate as many as three children in five will live in a single-parent household at some time. Among minorities the figures are even higher. In addition, the greatest incidence of poverty in the United States today is among single female parents and their children. Regardless of the actual figures, it is obviously a big problem in our society.

We cannot expect the best performance from students who are hungry, sickly, unloved and undisciplined. We cannot solve family problems completely in the classroom. In fact, most of the problems spill over from the youngsters who bring them to others who are in class primarily to learn. The socialization of the under-parented detracts from the education of all.

School authorities try in various ways to deal with these problem cases, but quite often it is the failing parent or parents who then object to the treatment of their children. They demand that their offspring be provided the education the law claims as their entitlement.

But having failed to provide the basic discipline to build self-discipline, which is the prime necessary ingredient for the process of education, they then object to proper school authorities providing that missing factor. The children that are denied at home the necessities for success are then denied the same from the educational system for the same reasons —- their parents.

Teachers are no less gifted than those of a generation ago, nor are they less well-trained. It is the parents that are different. These parents were the children who refused to be inconvenienced in any way for any cause or by any person or institution throughout their lives. Now, as the protectors and supposed benefactors of another generation, they once again seek convenience over effect, even to the detriment of their own children.

To be sure, most of the offenders do so for convenience, but some out of a false concern. These are the Dr. Spock parents who want to be pals to their children. With all due respect to Dr. (Benjamin)

Spock, a ten year old child does not need a thirty year old pal. A parent is more important than a friend.

A parent gives tenderness where there is pain, love where there is insecurity, guidance where there is error and discipline where there is failing. A parent, who cannot do all of these well, is not evil and probably not a bad parent. One who can do none of them should not have children.

Nevertheless, those parents who cannot provide all the support needed by their children should not deny the schools the occasion to fill in the gaps. So long as the children are not physically or emotionally harmed by the actions of their educators, the decisions on how to address their needs in the classroom should be left to those in authority in the school system.

If these problems are left unattended, they will take time and attention away from the main goal for the rest of the student body, that of learning. This cannot be allowed, as it destroys much of what our tax dollar is spent to achieve.

Discipline already takes an inordinate amount of our teachers' class time; this because of the severe limitations in recent years on the actions teachers and administrators can take to resolve student behavior problems. Paddling is out in many systems and in some states. So is any action which may humiliate or in any way lower the student's self-esteem.

It never occurs to those making these changes that the prime motivation for most human behavior, especially among the young, is to attract the approval of someone or some group. This may be parents, others in authority positions or peers.

If approval is not forthcoming, then fear, disgust, disapproval or any acknowledgment will be accepted as a substitute. Anything is better than to be ignored. Since some acknowledgment must be made, it is best to do something that will benefit the child. Discipline and guidance provided with obvious concern for the welfare of the student will do more good than expulsion or suspension.

There must come a time when schools are allowed to perform their function with the least interference from parents, save to insure that their children are not being abused and that they are receiving the education that is their due.

Having to wear proper clothing and to maintain an acceptable mode of appearance in accordance with a reasonable school code of dress and comportment is not abuse. It is not the inalienable right of a student to dress or conduct himself (or wear a hairstyle or jewelry) so as to distract others or himself from the mission —- to learn.

Ten or twenty years from now, when the student is engaged in some productive capacity in society, it will matter little how he or she was allowed to appear or dress while attending school, but it will mean quite a lot that an education was acquired that resulted in that later success.

Success in life depends largely on preparation, and that must be the mission of the parents and the schools. The nature of that preparation is at the center of the discussion in America concerning our education system, its function, its funding and its future. We must decide as a people what we want our schools to give to our children.

In the quarter of a century following World War II, we knew what to expect from schools, and we also knew what we expected of our children. The system was to teach our children to read and write, to do basic mathematics, to understand simple science, to appreciate art and music on an elementary level and to understand the importance of good health and exercise. The mission was simple, and it was executed fairly well.

We had a national campaign to keep potential drop-outs in school, and it was fairly successful. We encouraged all who could to go on to college, and a substantial number did. Our system appeared to be working very well. What went wrong?

What happened to change the system for the worse? Did families cease to prepare children for the education experience? Did families stop encouraging the students to excel? Did society change? Was the mission of the schools altered? Was there a significant change in the operation and functioning of the schools. Were the demands and expectations of life now different? Were the students of the new generation different from their parents? The answer to all of these is —- Yes!

Post-war parents saw education as a key to a brighter future, a future they could not hope for in their youth. They valued independence, especially from government assistance (and the supervision that accompanies it), and they knew that education would assure their children a degree of independence through career opportunities and personal achievement.

Today, many in our communities have been on various forms of government assistance for several generations. They are "controlled" by rules and regulations tied to their assistance, that actually prevent them from leaving the public support system.

If they leave, they have no medical benefits for their children or themselves. They may, in fact, have less money to live on, since they will have taxes to pay. They may also lose subsidies such as food stamps, rent and energy assistance, and other such supportive benefits.

The incentive to achieve academically for the children in such families, is overshadowed by their need to fill basic human needs, such as food, shelter and, often, love and support from absent parents. There are also many more families today in which the children are viewed as a burden, and they are subsequently unloved and unsupervised.

The result of the growth in the number of such families is that there are many more children coming to school with too little nourishment, too little encouragement, too little hope and too little intent to learn and succeed. They give up early, having seen their parents fail to reach any goals, if they ever had any.

They spend time in the system, but only to reach the point where they can leave. Many will continue the public support syndrome.

They will bring new children into the world to learn to live that life.

Some will enter vocations of crime because of the frustrations incurred from failure to qualify for mainstream jobs, or from the loss of such jobs, when they are unable to cope with the demands due to their lack of discipline they might have learned in school.

Those who stay in school will often disrupt or distract others from the tasks at hand and, thus, become a discipline problem for teachers, who must then take valuable class time away from education to attend to maintaining order. So, the changes in the family and the attitudes of parents have increased the number of students who enter school with little preparation or encouragement to learn and achieve.

And what of the changes in the demands of society as a whole? We can see much of these in the curriculum. How can we concentrate on turning out graduates skilled in math, science, language and the many technical abilities demanded by an increasingly complex employment market. We have even greater, more immediate needs for instruction on the prevention of teen pregnancy, sex education, facts about AIDS and other communicable diseases, abortion, gay and alternate lifestyles, cultural sensitivity.

It seems our children are too busy learning how to live with their fellow human beings and themselves socially to spare the proper mental and emotional energy achieving goals which affect their whole lives economically and personally, as well as their own children and families.

This is not to say there is no value in learning about these serious subjects, and there is certainly some urgency in addressing the problems that arise from ignorance of them in interpersonal relationships, but we must begin anew to stress the overwhelming importance of teaching students to master their own language together with math and science. But, how?

To solve this problem we will have to overcome the tragedy of broken homes, missing parents, neglectful parents, poverty and abuse. We will be forced to compete with electronic devices, television, movies and contemporary music to win the attention of those we seek to enrich. And we must instill allegiances stronger than the approval of our children's peers.

These are the forces that grab the attention of our young today. These are the distractions that pull their minds from that which will determine the richness of their future, and ours as a nation.

Electronic technology has developed so far over the past several decades that it comprises a whole category of distractions all by itself. A whole chapter could be written about its effects on every facet of our society today. But, on our children, it has been a draw against education, family, social relationships, economic activity, religion and every other part of their existence.

Kids play games, communicate with each other and family and institutions, as well as merchants, where they purchase so much with their enhanced purchasing power. Fortunately, advanced thinkers in education have developed ways to use technology in the education process. This has enabled schools to compete to some degree for the attention of their students.

This is an ongoing and developing process, so it will require constant innovation to continue the motivation of an easily distracted populace. So far, successes have been achieved, and there is hope for increased growth in that success.

Peer pressure, like the poor, will always be with us. Either we must direct each child to the "proper" group of peers, one that will apply the right pressures on the right issues and the right times, or we must seek to change the leadership make-up of each given group.

Usually, in any group, there is a leader. Sometimes it is the best person for the job, many times it is not. When we find a band that is listening to the wrong member, it is time to educate them to look to a new leader. We have to start teaching leadership skills to those we know will lead in the right directions.

This, too, can be done through the system. This may, in fact, be the way to increase the motivation of some to reach their study goals. School system psychologists fail when they do not develop programs to increase peer influence to help students reach acceptable levels of achievement.

Some think the way to compete with technology, theater and music is to entertain students into learning. There is no question that learning is easier when it is interesting, but subjects can be made interesting without being entertainment.

Children who are exposed to the excitement of learning at home are more likely to be motivated to learn at school. Studies have shown repeatedly that babies and toddlers have a voracious appetite for learning, and if it is encouraged, this attitude will continue throughout their entire lives. Perhaps we need courses in parenting, especially for first time parents.

It would be cheaper to teach parenting than to overcome the unnecessary mistakes of ill-informed new parents. Likewise, it is easier to teach teachers to stress the excitement and fun of learning their subject lessons over the subject matter itself than to rekindle the fire of learning that has been extinguished by boredom.

The biggest threat, however, to the learning attitude itself, is poor family environment. There are parents who do not love their children, who abuse them, who neglect them or just do not know how to care for them. A child who is not fed well cannot learn well. One without love and discipline and guidance at home will seek attention elsewhere, even if it is negative attention.

Children who feel no one cares about them will certainly rebel against the society they think has abandoned them. The American sense of personal freedoms and the sanctity of the private home and family has long kept us from interfering in such homes save to remedy physical abuse.

It can be argued that the changes in our society and in the American family warrant a review of this attitude, for it can be argued equally that, where children are concerned, lack of love or food or attention or proper care may constitute a form of abuse.

Even a lack of discipline can be abusive. Discipline does not necessarily mean physical punishment. Although an occasional whack on the backside, applied with love and concern, can have positive effects, there are other forms of discipline that are quite effective when used in the right circumstances and at the right times.

Parents who afford no discipline to their children deny them the preparation they need to meld effectively in modern society. Sometimes this occurs as a result of a misguided notion that they will be perceived by their children as mean or unloving. True parental love sometimes indicates action which will protect a child from future pain and sorrow.

Most of us at one time or another has heard a parent (probably our own) say, "This will hurt me more than you." or "This bothers me more than it does you." On the receiving end of the disciplinary action, these statements, of course, were of little comfort and may have seemed a bit disingenuous, but later in life we realized the value of the earlier course correction. Children need proper discipline in order to learn self-discipline, which is itself the basis for learning and for truly beneficial social relationships.

But, what of those who really do not care for their children, or who just refuse to endure the inconvenience required to practice good discipline in their household. We, as a society, cannot abandon these children to the whims or apathy of their parents, even if they are well-meaning.

If we take no action now, we will pay a price later. They will require our assistance through public welfare programs, or they will turn to crime. Either way, we pay. An ounce of prevention is still worth a pound of cure. Besides, the cure never really cures.

So what kind of prevention do we offer? How can we elicit correct discipline and proper care and involvement from parents who either don't know or don't want to know how to care for their children?

First, we must begin to demand certain levels of student behavior once again. There must be absolute prohibition and intolerance of certain kinds of behavior. Furthermore, students must be assured of swift and sure action by school authorities of serious breach of school codes of student conduct.

Discipline must be returned to the contemporary classroom in order to return to it the atmosphere of several decades ago when teachers ran the classrooms and tolerated no distractions from the mission of the class —- to learn.

Many will argue that this is impossible in light of today's attitudes toward personal liberties, not to mention modern court decisions across the nation asserting the rights of students to dress, appear and act as they wish with impunity. Legislatures across America must take the actions necessary to save a generation from their own immaturity. Our parents saved us, albeit in a different America, and we must save our own children from themselves.

Where there is a will, there is a way. We must return control of the classroom to the only adult usually present — the teacher. We already have the alternative.

Every school day across this country, there are students carrying weapons (guns and knives) to school, refusing directions of school authorities, threatening teachers or just telling them where to go. Not only are the offending children not learning, but the distractions are preventing others from learning as well.

In addition to returning discipline and order to the classroom, we need to involve parents more in the daily structuring of our children's lives. When a child seems unruly at school, there is probably a lack of discipline and guidance at home. Many parents spurn attempts by school authorities to involve them in solving their children's problems.

When called to come to the school to discuss difficulties or their children's progress or lack thereof, they avoid meeting with teachers or administrators, or they excuse themselves by attacking school personnel with charges of ineptitude or abuse. Some think their child's physical presence is their only obligation (some don't even insure that), and it is up to the school to persuade or cajole the child into learning.

If the student is not succeeding in school, it is the fault of the teachers, even though the parent will not encourage or require the student to complete the tasks assigned.

For parents such as these, a bigger "club" is necessary. School authorities need citation powers. If a parent refuses to come to school by appointment at reasonably convenient times, then the school should be able to cite the parent just as a police officer cites a motorist for failing to drive at the right speed or on the right side of the road.

A monetary fine is a powerful persuader. Further failure to look out for the interest of the child might result in arrest at home or at work. This would occur rarely, once it were recognized as a legitimate option of school authorities.

With parents attending meetings with school teachers and other staff, children would benefit from the new found interest of their parents. Behavior would improve; grades would improve; schools would improve. And, since success breeds further success, many students would far exceed their previous best performance levels.

What do we do, however, with those incorrigible parents, who refuse to be persuaded to act in their children's best interests? How can we help those children, who receive no love, guidance or attention from their parents? We, as a community, must act in their behalf.

Children living in an intolerable atmosphere, void of love, care and concern, should be removed and placed in an environment, where they will receive the tenderness, care and guidance necessary for them to realize their own dreams and future successes. Will it be costly? Yes, but far cheaper than prisons and welfare. But, does this mean more children's homes? No. Then, what?

When wealthy families have problem children, they send them to a military school instead of a prep school. Military schools are very expensive, and most average families could not possibly afford to follow that course of action. But the states can.

Each state could maintain a military academy or a system of academies in very large states. Youths who find it impossible to adapt to the structured atmosphere of public schools, and whose families will not provide them with the love and discipline to make that adaptation, would be taken from the negative situation at home and placed in the academy. The state would pay for it.

The student would now have some person or persons who care enough to wake the child up in the morning, provide a nutritious breakfast and make sure the child is in class on time and ready to learn. The student would have a clean and self-kept living area, and clean uniforms would be provided, thus instilling pride in appearance and living conditions.

Military discipline adapted to the particular age group would ensure structure and guidance to each child, and provide a sense of security, since each would understand what is required and guided to meet the requirements. Such training and discipline in addition to first rate education facilities would prove invaluable to any person, who, on graduation, would be entering the job market, college or even military service.

Back in the days of the draft, as in selective service, more than one draftee entered the military unwillingly, only to find he liked military life. Many stayed in the service and found a career. Why?

Because for many it was their first experience with success. They had never achieved much before entering the military. But, suddenly they were being appreciated. When they achieved a certain level of success, not only were they patted on the back for doing a good job, but they were rewarded with promotion and increased pay.

They were also entrusted with higher levels of responsibility. This was recognition of their worth as human beings. Someone acknowledged their importance, something they had never experienced in civilian life.

Military structure can bring out abilities many never knew they had. A military academy might similarly help youths who have never had the opportunity to succeed. And success breeds an appetite for further success.

We as a nation cannot allow such children to fall prey to their own circumstances. If we allow them to fall through the cracks, if we allow them to fail through our own apathy, then their failure will become our failure, and we will pay dearly for it. Such failures often compound, and the payment compounds as well, especially when it is paid much later.

To address payment and education, one must look at today's schools in America from the organizational view. In most states the system divides into local school districts. There are various forms of funding, but most are inefficient and insufficient.

The worst local systems require local boards of education to raise money to fund a substantial amount of the budget. Larger states have hundreds of these local boards and are heavily burdened by the cost of administrative bureaucracies, thus reducing the amount available for the raison d'etre of the system —- education.

Whether funded by property taxes (archaic and unfair), sales taxes (regressive) or income taxes (probably the most reasonable source), education in today's society is not a local concern and cannot be handled efficiently on the local level. It is a societal and national concern and must be addressed by a structure high enough for an unclouded view of the problems and the solutions.

There is today a growing discussion of using vouchers as a way to improve our system by encouraging competition among school districts. There are valid arguments on both sides of the issue. The right of parents to decide which schools can best serve the needs of their children is the foremost logic in favor of the proposal.

Parents are paying taxes to support education, therefore, it seems reasonable that they should be able to choose their best option for their own children. The government would simply process the money and send it to the schools selected by the parents.

On the other hand, we might also jeopardize some schools, especially those in inner city areas, by drawing away many fine students, thus leaving only those too poor or those who for other reasons cannot attend some other districts. The resulting diminished student population of those schools and the corresponding lower funding would further erode the remaining quality of education.

It can also be said that a voucher system is the most direct admission that our public school system is failing. The competition among our schools might help, or it might simply make things worse. The growth of charter schools over the last two decades have made that point. But competition here is not the only measure of success.

To compete on an international level, as we must today, we need to look at what other countries are doing in education. In Germany, for instances, all personnel in education are state employees. The "local" area just provides the physical plant. This certainly saves resources over a system such as ours.

Japan, like most European countries, has tiered education. Not all students are going to college, therefore, not all need a college preparatory course of study. Some need technical training. Some need vocational preparation. Why does the American system offer generic education? Why don't we prepare our children for the future they want?

Why should a child who wants to be a carpenter not be prepared to enter the field at high school level as an apprentice? Why can't a student who wants to be a mechanic or a cosmetologist be given the concentrated schooling to enter the field directly on graduation? Some schools are doing that, but it is hardly commonplace.

Perhaps we should test and counsel our children after the eighth grade to direct them to the correct high school, a high school specializing in the kind of area, technical field or discipline (there's that word again) that draws their career interests.

Whatever we decide as a nation, our education system needs an overhaul. We have a system now that was designed in the nineteenth century, refined in the middle of the twentieth century and should be completely rebuilt to address the needs of the twenty-first century.

We cannot drop a computerized electronically controlled, turbocharged modern engine into a Model T, and expect it to meet our needs. It is time to buy a new vehicle to carry our children into the future we want for them. Maybe it is too much to entrust to a government structure we no longer believe can even balance a budget. But that's another topic.

HEALTH CARE IN AMERICA

The health of nations is more important than the wealth of nations.

Will Durant 1885-1981

The health of the people is really the foundation upon which all their happiness and all their powers as a state depend. (Speech July 24, 1877)

British Prime Minister

Benjamin Disraeli

1804-1881

Health care is one of the most prominent topics in America today. The Clinton Administration made universal access to health care a cornerstone of its term. But the Obama Administration, with the help of a Congress controlled by Democratic allies, finally passed the Affordable Care Act, or Obamacare in 2010.

Health is one of the most personal issues in every person's life. Health and health care affect almost everything we do and every decision we make. Our jobs, our hopes, our families, our future as individuals, all rely on the state of our health and the care we can depend on, when we are ill.

It is a special concern for all those millions in America today who have no health care at all or very inadequate care, although millions of Americans have obtained coverage under the new program.

We on the bottom have known for many years that such a system as existed in the U.S. prior to the ACA was unacceptable in such a rich and developed nation. We have our own ideas on the present state of health care availability in this country, what has brought us to this point, and where we should be headed. We even have some notions on how we might get there.

Throughout the ages, from the time of Greek scholars and Asian philosophers to Roman poets and European statesmen up to modern-day moralists and politicians, only food and sex have been discussed, debated and manipulated more than health care in seeking contentment, control or just raw power. Interestingly, these are exactly parallel to the basic human life necessities of nourishment, affection and health.

The scholars have studied them; the philosophers have explored their true meanings; the poets have sung about them; the statesmen have used and misused all of them from time to time; the moralists decry their scarcity and abuse in the name of all that is right, while the politicians promise each and all to attain their noble as well as ignoble ends.

Food is a fundamental concern in a discussion of the economy, and sex is central to any serious dialogue on morals and family. Health, or, more specifically, health care, is a matter of severe importance in modern America, not only for families, not only as relates to the economy, but in almost every area affecting the inhabitants of this nation. Health care is perhaps THE topic in the United States. Just ask any Republican running for national office.

Americans have been accustomed to stories in the media about people across the country in need of advanced medical treatments that are very expensive and unavailable to them because they lack the financial resources to pay for them. Financial resources, to most Americans, means health insurance.

Those who have good insurance have access to the best medical care in the world. Those who do not generally receive care that ranks not much higher than that available in some third world countries. In matters involving health care we have been a nation of two classes —- the haves and the have-nots, that is, those who have insurance and those who do not. For those who lack this all important commodity fear can be a daily companion.

Before the ACA – A little girl of five needs a bone marrow transplant. Not only must she wait and hope for a donor, she must wait for her parents' pleas for help to raise tens of thousands of dollars for the down payment for the surgery and treatment. Her life may be over before it ever really begins. Her parents wait, hope and plead for help, and they worry. This kind of life should not be found in America.

Before the ACA – A man in his mid-40's needs kidney surgery as well as other medical care. He is self-employed in a modest business and cannot obtain health insurance due to long existing health problems. He was formerly elected to public office and for a time was covered under a group insurance policy which ceased to cover him when he left office. He had medical procedures performed while he was under that coverage, but now he needs more, and the coverage is gone. His only avenues are a series of small payments over many years to doctors and hospitals or —- bankruptcy.

Now, both of these scenarios can be avoided almost always.

And how about the stories we have all heard of the older Americans who are living on dog food or worse because of the cost of their medication. They have to choose between food and prescriptions. The addition of Part D to Medicare helped these situations greatly, but there are still some elderly caught in this trap.

There are also those who have been forced to divorce their spouses in order to receive the public aid needed to obtain medical care for their sick marital partners or risk losing everything they have spent a lifetime earning on one catastrophic illness. This problem still follows us.

The problem, simply stated, was that in America young, old and those in between were in danger of losing their health and, indeed, their lives due only to the inaccessibility of a grotesquely monstrous medical system. The health care system in modern America is one of the best equipped, most technically advanced and most competently staffed in the world.

It was, unfortunately, also one of the least accessible, especially to those at the bottom of the economic ladder. Such was the state of medical care and medicine: the best there is for the rich, very good care for the average person, and the very least for those who seem to need it most and most often.

Then came the Affordable Care Act. Is it the perfect answer? No. Is it an improvement? Absolutely! Since the time of Theodore Roosevelt, political leaders have called for a system that would bring accessibility of health care to all Americans. Both Presidents Nixon and Clinton pushed for even more comprehensive coverage, but could not get Congress to approve their ideas.

The principal problem with the American health care system was that the entire medical establishment was practically control free. There were few real government controls, only a facade for professional association controls and no real market control. The result was a monopoly.

Doctors don't really compete with one another. Pharmaceutical companies don't compete in areas of price and quality. Hospitals, likewise, seem to serve special needs or geographic areas rather than consumer demand for competition.

The bureaucracy of government does more to slow delivery of new medical products than to encourage cost control. And cost is the wall that barred almost a third of our population from access to most health care.

The greatest cost by far is, for most of us, the physician. Once the most respected member of most communities, the doctor is seen today by many as a greedy, uncaring opportunist who feeds off the pain and discomfort of others only to retire to wealth and comfort.

That may not be exactly a true characterization of most doctors, and people may not feel that way about "my own doctor", but it certainly illustrates the attitude of many Americans toward the medical profession as a whole. And there is unquestionably enough publicly available information to support such feelings.

The American Medical Association through its medical professors, who staff all the medical schools, keep the price of medical education and the limited number of schools and classes at a level that discourages the proliferation of medical doctors and, thereby, limits the supply of medical care.

Add to this the fact that more and more physicians choose to attain advanced training and specialize rather than serve as a general practitioner. After all, there is a lot more money in gynecology or cardiology than there is in appendectomies and tonsillectomies.

There are now more doctors specializing in such high priced care than there are those interested in family medical care. The greatest need now is the good old family doctor, but nobody wants to be one.

Why specialize? If your heart is failing, you have no choice but to see a cardiologist. Since there is no choice, and since they all charge such inflated fees, you go, you bite the bullet and pay the price, and you do without other things you may need. At least you stay alive.

And that is the crux of the problem. When the doctor is "selling" you your life, what price is too high? Many must do without the essentials of decent living, sometimes even food, in order to afford such specific types of health care. And, for those without any insurance, there is no such choice available. They simply do without the care they need.

Many have conditions that deteriorate to disability or even death, a death that need not have been, but nonetheless, often welcome for the sake of alleviating their pain. Life should not be for sale.

The doctor is really in no position to change this. After medical school, most doctors are saddled with hundreds of thousands of dollars of debt. Added to those payments are the cost of setting up practice. Then there is the medical malpractice insurance. The total cost of debt, insurance, equipment and staff require a doctor to work long hours and see little actual reward for twenty or thirty years. Then they can start saving for retirement.

Oh, for the days when, as we see in old movies, the family doctor would come to the house to comfort and heal the sick even sometimes in the dead of night. And the cost — a few dollars; or a cake or a cut of beef, or maybe even nothing if the family was of modest means. That is not to say that doctors didn't make a decent living, or that they worked for practically nothing.

They had plenty of patients and also, fortunately, plenty of patience for those whose needs were not always timed perfectly with their ability to pay. Modern demands have played a role in the disappearance of the home visit.

The number of patients a doctor must serve, the need for complex instruments and equipment, and the greatest culprit of all (certainly in the minds of doctors), malpractice litigation, have joined to discourage American doctors from taking the time and the risk of treating patients in a home environment.

This is not to say this service is unavailable elsewhere in the world. In most accessible places it is still a thriving form of care. And recently, there has been a revival of the practice here in America. It's not everywhere, but it is growing.

(Some years ago, while on a business trip to Europe, I caught a virus while staying in Monte Carlo. It was April, and I found that this is a common occurrence among visitors to the area. When the hotel was advised that I was not feeling well, they asked if I needed a doctor. I told them I would appreciate seeing a doctor, but it was Sunday, and I did not think one would be available.

Twenty minutes later a doctor knocked at my door. He examined me and wrote four prescriptions. The cost was sixty dollars for the prescriptions, including the hotel employee picking them up at the drugstore, and one hundred and twenty dollars for the doctor visit to the hotel room on a Sunday. This kind of service is common in Europe.

Author)

While Americans feel shortchanged on services by their physicians, they are truly gouged by the pharmaceutical industry. Americans pay outrageous prices for their prescription drugs, more than any other nationality in the world.

There can be no plausible explanation for paying more for the same drugs, and, yet, that is the case, no matter what drug we seem to be discussing. The drug companies say this is not true, or they say they are simply recapturing their research and development cost.

There are many drugs, however, that have been around for decades, the development costs regained a thousand times, and, still, Americans pay more for them than our neighbors elsewhere in the world.

Americans in Buffalo, Detroit and other cities on our northern border routinely buy their drugs in Canada for just one reason. The prices are significantly lower. Unfortunately, most of us have no such easy access. There is no excuse for such wide variances in prescription prices. The only answer is greed.

There seems to be no conscience in the boardrooms of the American pharmaceutical industry. Older Americans faced with needs for life-sustaining prescriptions and limited means resort to eating dog food, turning their heat down or even off in winter, or living on the streets.

But the industry continues to report record profits, and they continue to spend more money on promoting their products than any other industry proportionately. Their marketing representatives are among the best compensated in American business circles. And their marketing expense accounts are generous to not only the representatives themselves but also their customers, the doctors, hospitals and drugstore chains upon whom they lavish tremendous gifts and perqs to persuade them to stock or prescribe the prescription products they hawk.

And who pays for these extra benefits? Why, the poor sap at the end of consumer chain —- US. While the pharmaceutical industry and their customers feast on the champagne dinner, we get the cork and the tab.

Again, however, it is the government we elect to protect us that not only allows this fleecing to continue, it actually contributes to the problem. The Food and Drug Administration routinely delays life saving drugs from reaching the market for years after their development.

The agency is supposed to investigate each new drug to insure it has been properly tested for safety and effectiveness before it is approved for public use in the United States, but the record shows that the process is not only slow and unresponsive to public health needs, but it is often not even effective at insuring safety.

The thalidomide debacle of several decades ago is the best example of the failure that can occur in this agency. Many babies were born with horrible deformities that were to make their lives unalterably miserable, just because this drug was approved for use by pregnant women without adequate testing.

There have been other drugs whose testing was questionable before their approval by the FDA, and the resulting use by doctors and their patients unaware of the potential for problems, has been a nightmare for many.

At the same time, the FDA has held up or stopped the use of prescription drugs that are used safely in other countries, sometimes for many years, with no problems and with a reputation for alleviating suffering.

The medical community and pharmaceutical industry, even joined by bumbling bureaucratic agencies, are not the only culprits in this charade we call the American health care system. One of the biggest cost items in medical care has nothing to do with health, care or even science.

The cost of malpractice insurance is staggering when compared with insurance costs for almost any other business. This cost is a major chunk of every medical bill in America. It is not high because the insurance companies just want to make a "big profit", although many medical people probably think that is the case.

Premiums reflect the ever increasing cost of litigation itself, including the cost of lawyers, their time in court and in legal research, court costs and the twentieth century phenomenon which is the jury award of punitive damages. These awards can sometimes be millions of dollars and are in no way connected to the loss suffered by the victim, but are supposed to reflect somehow the degree of fault of the medical care provider.

As a result of awards of insane amounts in punitive damages, insurance companies charge significantly higher premiums for malpractice coverage. These costs in turn are passed on to patients in the form of higher fees.

But that is not the end of the chain. Doctors, in order to keep the premiums from being even higher seek to satisfy the insurance carriers admonishments to exercise more "care" in their treatments, often run more tests on a patient than may be actually necessary in order to make sure they have "covered all the bases" in case the treatment fails, or they miss a hidden symptom, and the suffering patient or a relative later sues for negligence.

This, in turn, places more pricing demands on the patient or on the patient's insurance, resulting in increased premiums for the patient's medical insurance. So, everyone gets to pay for malpractice awards, or more specifically for punitive damage awards.

Many would say that a patient may well deserve a million or so for the pain and suffering caused by a "careless" physician, but let's be realistic for a moment. Some of these patients will never get to use any of the money. Still others will see very little added to their lives from the money. Even their families, who certainly share in their pain and grief, will receive little comfort from these substantial funds.

The lawyers will often take one third in addition to expenses and costs, leaving sometimes less than half for the injured party. Often the funds end up with children or other family members, who while losing some of the companionship they might have received from their loved one, suffered little by comparison.

And one could hardly argue for the potential earnings the injured party will not receive as a result of the loss. Not many would have earned in the millions, and tax free. So, who wins? The legal system. Who loses? Not the doctors and hospitals; they pass it on. Not the insurance companies; they pass it on. We lose.

The average American pays for the extra tests, the increased premiums, the increased fees, the taxes that run the courts; in short, we pay the whole tab.

Even the hospitals cost more than they should. It seems almost every hospital in America wants to be all things to all patients. Hospitals seem always to be building a "new wing" or adding a CAT scanner or an MRI system.

They don't want to send a patient and his money to a competitor for expensive tests, so they buy all the new expensive hardware and beef up their own laboratories in order to keep those dollars at home. But this also means they have to make a big initial outlay to purchase the state of the art equipment and hire new personnel to operate it.

These costs are once again passed on to each and every patient who may use a particular hospital, even those who don't need the advanced care systems. It is also passed on the patients' health care insurance companies, who in turn raise premiums in the area served by the hospital. Again, the American public pays the price.

The staggering costs of doctors, medicines, hospital care, medical equipment, insurance and legal procedures involved in health care in America make one of the costliest parts of life in this nation, but the cost does not stop there. The ripple effect is even more menacing to anyone who considers all the related consequences of not having a system that serves everyone efficiently and economically.

Consider the welfare system in the United States. Some have estimated that as many as seventy percent of those on public assistance programs in this country could and would leave it to work in low paying jobs, if only they did not have to worry about health care for themselves or for their children.

Many jobs that go begging would be filled. Many who are on assistance programs would find fulfillment in self-sufficiency. Many children would be given opportunities to mature in an atmosphere nurturing self-esteem and self-reliance. The rolls of those receiving tax dollars would shift to millions paying taxes.

Government deficit spending would reduce possibly to the point of national debt reduction, assuming also that we begin electing smarter, more ethical leaders. At any rate, one of the most costly segments of our national and state budgets would be reduced to what it was intended to be —- a temporary safety net.

As an example, we can look at Niagara Falls. Niagara Falls, Ontario, is bustling with activities for tourists. There are stores, shops, boutiques; big businesses and small businesses. Many are owned by the Provincial Park system, but there are a great number of small, mom and pop type shops that sell souvenirs or snacks, and they make a good living, although not enough to pay for an expensive health care plan.

Fortunately, they don't have to worry about that. The government takes care of all health care claims. They pay for it through a national services tax, which is added onto every product and service in Canada, like an extra sales tax.

By contrast, on the U.S. side in Niagara Falls, New York, there is blight, urban blight. Run down homes in run down neighborhoods with poor people and few if any businesses. Why? No health care is one big reason.

Many of the people in those neighborhoods could and probably would work in businesses similar to those in Canada for the tourists, but they have no resources to start them, and they can't afford to buy their own health insurance. We should be able to compete in such a small market with such a tremendous tourist industry. There is some evidence the ACA is having a positive effect in alleviating this problem. Time will tell.

And what of our ability to compete in the world market place. We have been hurt by cheap producers in the world who have an advantage. Some countries provide total health care from government resources, leaving the industries with no expense for employee medical needs.

The result is lower business costs in the production of their goods, and lower prices. Our manufacturers cannot possibly compete head to head with other developed nations which, in effect, subsidize their industries. Hence our loss of leadership in many fields. And the loss of that leadership has meant the loss of American jobs, national income and the ability of the United States to cope with its own economic needs as a nation.

Our national debt and recurring annual deficit bear witness to our economic losses worldwide, although defense costs have been a major drain as well.

We have built the most capable and best equipped medical system in the world, but, unfortunately, we have done it in a haphazard and patchwork way. The end result is a system with the facility to serve anyone with the best humanity can offer, but with the real ability to serve only a large segment of our society.

A nation as great as this and with the facilities and abilities that are available here, is a failure if it fails to serve any one of its members. We must move into the ranks of the other developed nations of the world and build a system of medical care that serves every member of our society. If England can do it, if Germany can do it, if Japan can do it, and if Russia can do it, America can do no less.

For many years, discussion has centered on the Canadian system or the English system, their shortfalls and benefits, whether either would work in the United States with its very different social mix. Some, especially the insurance industry oppose either for obvious reasons. Such a system as either would negate the need for insurance companies in the health field, since the government would be the sole provider of health insurance.

But what about the system used in Germany. Since 1917 Germany has had essentially the same system, and it seems to work quite well. Everyone in Germany has good health care. The people are happy with the system. The medical community is happy with the system. The insurance industry seems happy with the system. And the government is quite comfortable with the current system. Any health care system that can satisfy apparently everyone is one worth examining and possibly copying or adapting for American use.

It appears that, periodically, the government, the medical industry and the insurance industry meet to set the parameters for the system. They arrive at agreements on what medical procedures and services will be available at what cost and how it will all be managed. The government taxes and pays for the programs. The insurance industry administers the payments, and, of course, the medical institutions provide the services.

Since all is arrived at by agreement, all the parties are content to play their part at agreed upon prices (even the doctors) and under agreed upon arrangements. Laws necessary to govern the distribution and administration of services and medicines are passed as needed by the government. Prices are strictly controlled and enforced. New drugs are approved as rapidly as testing will allow. In short, the medical needs of the people are the prime concern for all.

Everyone knows that care is available to all, and the use of facilities, equipment and personnel by everyone spreads the cost over the whole population, not just those who can afford it. Everyone benefits; everyone pays. In our system everyone pays, but a significant portion of our population has been denied access to the system they need as much as everyone else.

It is too bad that the politicians are not among those in need of health insurance. Perhaps, if they were, we might have expected faster action to remedy this problem. Members of Congress have wonderful coverage, the best available. So they have had little incentive to do much more than debate over who has the best or worst idea.

Meanwhile, there were so many who had to wait on their folly. Some ran out of time, before our leaders ran out of wind. It seems everyone has a chance to suffer, except those who are supposed to be curing the illness. Finally, they passed the Affordable Care Act. It is not the perfect solution, but it is a start.

Sadly, the Republicans in Congress and running for President seem bent on dismantling the only attempt to fix a badly broken system. They have no ideas for replacing it, so they would destroy the only access millions now have. If anything the ACA needs improvement. It needs expansion in its scope and more to address the actual cost of care.

As a nation, we Americans must take care of our neighbors, for we may need them in a crisis, and, besides, it's the right thing to do. In a nation as great and gifted as this, no one should want for food or appreciation or for just good health.

We are a people endowed by our creator with certain inalienable rights, among which are life, liberty and the pursuit of happiness. Life should not be a gift to those who can afford the price, no matter how high. Those who are in poor health cannot truly pursue their own happiness. And who is really free whose life is deteriorating for lack of adequate care.

Just as a chain is only as strong as its weakest link, we as a nation can be only as strong as those we care for the least. The wealth of our country is certainly linked to the health of its people —- all its people.

RAGS TO RICHES.....TO RAGS?

Three Generations in the U.S. Economy

The Great Depression, like most other periods of severe unemployment, was produced by government mismanagement rather than by any inherent instability of the private economy.

Milton Friedman

Capitalism and Freedom (1962)

Depression, boom, recession, the rise of labor unions and the flight of manufacturing facilities, first from the industrial North and, then, from America itself. These have defined the economy of the United States throughout most of the last century and into this one. The average American feels almost helpless in facing the rollercoaster that is the American economy.

As individuals, we have very little effect on the circumstances that guide our economic life as a nation. The institutions that control the major factors of economic import are sometimes our masters. If it is true that America was built by individuals, that is, by many strong individual persons, then, it must be at least somewhat true that the American economy of today was built by using individuals with little regard for the welfare of those who were used, those on the bottom.

Big business and even big labor (leaders) have used those on the bottom to achieve their own ends, often without a thought or care of what are the futures of those on the bottom and their communities, or, for that matter, their country. The biggest problem, however, is our government, the one institution designed specifically to protect our interest.

Our government seems unable to control our economy, incapable of supervising the other institutions that do control it and even unable to balance one annual national budget in several decades until the late 1990's. How did such a mess arise? Who let it happen? What do we on the bottom expect our leaders to do to fix the problem?

In ancient times it was said that all roads led to Rome. Today it could just as easily be said in the United States that all problems can be traced to the economy. The breakdown of the family in America is due in part to the changes in our economic system.

The failure of the system is blamed for a great deal of the growth of crime nationally. Greed, avarice, injustice, bigotry, suicides, depression, medical problems, almost anything bad in this society today is connected in some way to the transition of the American economy over the past several decades. The financial health of America, still among the economic titans of the world, is cause for concern in many quarters of this country as we still transition from the last century to the new one.

The mere fact, however, that the troubles of our society can be traced to the economy does not necessarily mean that the economy is the cause. It is actually just another problem, a symptom of some underlying illness of modern America.

When the last century began, Americans were still in a celebrating mood left over from the gay nineties, which were themselves, the celebration of the end of the recession of the eighties. The United States was enjoying the prosperity of the industrial revolution.

People were living exceptionally well by the standards of the nineteenth century, and a vibrant economy meant that more and more were enjoying the fruits of the boom. As the economy of the nation shifted from its traditional agricultural base to the new urban manufacturing one, people poured into the cities in droves.

This growth continued with minor pauses until well after the First World War, an event that even fueled the furnace of American industrial growth, while, at the same time, catapulting the United States into its new position as a world leader. But, as Americans found out too late, such a meteoric rise to such astronomical heights can bring a devastating fall, when there is no firm foundation for the seeming free ride to success.

And there was no foundation for the economic juggernaut of the roaring twenties. There was no real experience with the stock market. Stocks were not well understood by those who sold them, let alone an average American. And there was no Securities Exchange Commission or any other government agency to offer protection from unregulated charlatans, or just untrained peddlers.

A society drunk at the party of success took a wild ride on this new roller coaster, the stock market, thrilled by the up's and down's, since the up's were more numerous and steeper than the down's. Little did they expect the horrible hangover at the end of the last, steep drop that ended the ride.

The stock market crash of 1929 and the depression that followed it left America in financial ruin. More than one quarter of Americans were left without work of any kind. Millions lost their homes, their possessions, everything. Farmers lost farms that had been in their families for generations. Manufacturers closed their plants and laid off workers who had no other skills and nowhere else to go even if they did.

Our history books and our older Americans tell us how a courageous generation led by the right leader for the right time, Franklin D. Roosevelt, and helped immeasurably by a wartime economy, fought their way not only to victory in World War II, but to a bigger victory for their economic survival as a nation. The result shot America to the top of the international economic heap.

The United States was now not just a world leader, but THE world leader; strongest militarily and strongest economically.

Our economy was strong, but at what price? Many have criticized the New Deal programs of FDR for saddling the United States with the first real debt it had ever known as a nation. Certainly the U.S. had borrowed before, and it had a modest debt, but nothing that could not be paid off with any small frugality.

But the New Deal brought a national debt in the many billions of dollars. Unfortunately, there was no other way. This country was in danger for its very existence. There was growing discontent that actually threatened anarchy. If this unique concept in government that involved the people in their own rule was to survive, something had to be done, and it had to be done quickly.

The only way was to borrow money to stimulate the economy, and, at the same time, supply the necessities of life to all who needed help until they could once again sustain themselves. That was the beginning of government involvement in the machinery of our societal economy, and it was the beginning of the welfare system of today.

It is also the reason America rose like a phoenix from the ashes of economic ruin to become the world power of today. The generation that survived the Depression, especially the children, is the same generation that won the Second World War, and it is the same generation that found the greatest prosperity the world has ever known in the period after that war.

These were the men and women that built the auto industry that prompted the phrase, "what's good for General Motors is good for America." These were the people who built the rubber and steel industries, and who created the plastics industry. This generation of Americans built the breadbasket of America so that it could help feed the world. They rose from the rags of the Depression to the relative riches of the post-War period.

By comparison, the Recession of 2008 was an inconvenience. But our experience in the Great Depression at least prepared us for the hard decisions we would have to make as a nation following the 2008 economic collapse. And once again, it turned out what was good for General Motors was good for America.

But to return to events that saved us from the Drpression, from a stock market in ruin came a new regulated market that purveyed stocks of value for value, and the market flourished. Interest rates were low enough to stimulate the growth of the economy while paying a reasonable profit to those who managed America's money. Unemployment was low as was inflation, with only minor occasional recessions.

Our national debt rose, but only modestly, and everyone assumed we would be in a position to pay it off in a few years. America was comfortable with this wondrous economy that seemed to offer success to everyone who would work for it.

There was some friction, however, since labor unions and management in many industries had never really buried the hatchet from their earlier days of confrontation. From the early part of that century, there was a reluctance of management leaders to acquiesce to the demands of labor leaders for more security, pay and benefits for American workers.

Labor unions formed in order to give strength of numbers to workers who needed the security of job protection from sometimes over-demanding supervisors, who could fire or otherwise punish workers often without cause and usually without oversight. Workers wanted reasonable pay and benefits for themselves and their families.

Brutal means were used to subdue worker unrest, often resulting in violent confrontations that left many injured and some dead. Only government intervention in the form of new laws to protect workers' rights, especially the right to collective bargaining, saved these clashes from degenerating to a civil war.

Today, it is recognized here that labor is a resource and must be valued as is any other resource. There are still labor-management disputes, but they are settled at the bargaining table or in the courts. Since the 1960's, organized labor has steadily declined in membership. Many said they were no longer necessary due to new laws protecting workers.

In the 50's, labor was at its peak in numbers and in power. Still industry here was the envy of the world. We built a middle class and hope for every American that such a status was within reach of everyone. Still, because of the flourishing economy and in spite of a marginal tax rate in the ninety percentile range, the rich got richer. Everyone seemed to be doing well by world standards. But as labor declined, so did everyone. Except the wealthy!

It can be said that American managers still don't consult enough with their employees, and, because of this, many opportunities to improve efficiency and productivity are missed. One need only study the success of Japanese managers to see the benefit of using the knowledge of workers to the best advantage of business.

And labor unions have their problems as well, the most troubling of which is probably the disappearance of the great, selfless and able labor leader of yesterday. Gone are the George Meany's, the John L. Lewis's and even the Jimmy Hoffa's. The union leader of today is as likely to be serving self-interest as to be looking out for the interest of the members.

And the national labor leaders just don't have the ability or even the character of the old time battling street fighters of the formative years of organized labor. Most of today's labor leaders are more like executives, who are simply managing a new industry, whose product is labor. They negotiate to get the best price and other compensation for their "product". They are no different from the management people they face across the table.

Management in America today is a different story. If labor's leadership has become like management, management has become like a separate government without territory. U.S. industry seems to have forsaken their roots in favor of greater profits. There is no loyalty today among American industries for the nation that spawned them, for the mother country that nurtured them or for the workers that built them. We should have seen it coming long ago.

For decades American companies have moved into communities, grown with the support of local residents, profited from the labors of local workers, and then left the communities high and dry when they found new less costly environments elsewhere. Perhaps utilities were cheaper, or labor was cheaper, or labor was not organized, or there were lower taxes.

For a few dollars these observers of only the bottom line would cut the economic throats of their erstwhile loyal hosts, pull up stakes and hit the road to greener, or should we say more golden, pastures.

Many times a local industry, possibly family owned, was bought by a large company in the same business. This would reduce competition and produce profits that would return the investment in just a few years. In all honesty, it would also spread costs and usually make the business more profitable.

Often some of the production assignments would be transferred to other company facilities elsewhere in the country in the name of improved efficiency and specialization. Sometime later, when changes in the marketplace dictate a reduction of facilities or personnel, the company closes the facility that is most limited or least efficient, and that usually turns out to be the old facility that was bought some time back in that small community.

Now the employees, many of whom have been loyal members of the team for life, even generations, are out of a job and, maybe, out of a livelihood altogether. Their hard work meant nothing; their loyalty meant nothing —- bottom line!

In addition, instead of the shareholders reaping the new profits, more often than not, the executive or management team would receive bonuses or incentives that would eat up the additional profits. Even if the company loses money, the board finds a way to "reward" the CEO and his team.

Of course, the board is made up of CEO's from other companies. They take care of a team member, because he sits on some of their boards, and he will remember this gesture when their raises come up. The most needed improvement at the SEC is for oversight protection of shareholders' rights.

If American industry has no allegiance to communities across the country full of loyal workers and supportive local institutions, or even their own shareholders, how could we expect them to bear any allegiance to our country? For decades they have been milking the system of tax breaks, government incentives, grants and almost anything that might increase the bottom line, with little consideration for the overall health and well-being of this nation, except insofar as their profits are affected.

The only time American industry seems to wave the red, white and blue is when it increases the green. And, yet, our own government seems bent on helping big business move every good-paying job out of the country until the vast majority of Americans are working for minimum wage.

And the minimum wage has stagnated for decades. Based on the minimum wage set in the 60's, today's should be over $17 an hour. And yet, Congress doesn't even consider it for change. Even raising it to $15 would raise millions out of poverty, and there would be additional benefits.

For many, there would be no further need of food stamps, resulting in large sums saved by the federal government. In addition, these workers would be paying more into Social Security and Medicare funds, shoring them up for years. Many would also begin paying federal and state taxes, bringing more revenue and reducing deficit spending.

Add to all this the additional spending, and the economy itself gets a huge boost. Also, if those on the bottom get raises, it will force all other wage levels to rise. More money into the economy brings more robust growth. Will prices go up? Of course, but the stimulation of the economy will provide growth to offset the need for huge increases. We will grow overall faster than inflation. There are greater threats.

American companies receive credit toward their U.S. taxes for taxes paid to foreign governments. That invites relocation. Why wouldn't they move? If they can find labor for five dollars a day, locations with no government oversight of environmental impact, little local taxation and full credit against their U.S. taxes, and still claim to be American companies with all the national benefits enjoyed by such "American" companies, they would be financially foolish not to take advantage of the situation.

But industry did not create this incentive to leave, our government did. The people we elected to protect our best interest have sold us out for a better deal. But the better deal is for them, not us.

We don't have the money to invest in our elected officials' campaign funds. Big business and other special interests have ready funds to pour into the coffers of any "helpful" politician who can assist them in improving their profitability, even if it is at the expense of working Americans and their families and communities. The impact spreads like a contagious disease.

Families of unemployed or underemployed (taking a job at minimum wage to have some income) workers need public assistance. That means we all get to pay more taxes. We subsidize the businesses. The local community loses tax base and must then either increase local taxes or cut services. Now we all pay more or lose our safety or neighborhood.

Additionally, local schools lose tax revenues. They then must reduce personnel and offer a less comprehensive education to our children. Less education usually means less productivity and success later in life. We can now pass our economic woes on to another generation.

And the ripples continue to neighboring communities and on the state and national levels in the forms of higher taxes, lower services, lower economic bases at every level and increased crime. And when criminal activity increases, more of our resources must be diverted to protection and prosecution. This compounds the shortage of resources available for other government services, and the cycle continues.

The undermining of America's industrial employment is not the only economic sin of government in the United States. Our national debt is over seventeen trillion dollars and growing fast, fuelled by a perennial budget deficit created and perpetuated by incompetent or unscrupulous leaders in a Congress that, as an institution, long ago ceased to be responsive to the needs of the average American.

In the late 90's, bipartisan cooperation balanced the budget and produced a surplus for two years in a row. They even paid down some of the national debt. But an incoming administration along with Congress decided to reduce federal revenues by means of a huge tax cut. Supposedly, that would stimulate the economy and boost new job creation.

It was the seventh time that tactic had been used since the Kennedy Administration. It never worked the other six times, and it didn't work this time either. But that tax cut, along with two wars that were never funded and a major change in Medicare benefits, also unfunded, drove the economy headlong into the Recession of 2008. So much for the wisdom of leadership.

Those of us on the bottom feel especially estranged from those elected to high federal office to secure our interests as a people. Almost everyone in America today outside of politics can see the distance growing between our leaders and the people they are elected to represent. It may not be long before we are all political astronomers wondering at the seeming light years between ourselves and the "stars" in Washington.

Every administration since FDR has had to contend with problems in the economy, but during the post-war period they were never so acute as they have been from the mid-seventies until today. The last balanced budget was produced by the Clinton Administration and a GOP led Congress. No other post World War II president before or since has been able to come even close to balancing a budget.

During Richard Nixon's second term and Gerald Ford's succession to it, inflation became such a problem that Ford trumped up his WIN (whip inflation now) effort, which was ill-conceived and apparently ineffective.

Jimmy Carter took over and was so weak in his economic policy that the entire economy of the United States went into overload. Interest rates rose to new outrageous heights; inflation reached double digits; unemployment was higher than at any time since the depression.

Americans were so disgusted with the mismanagement of this nation's financial resources that they were an easy target for the Ronald Reagan campaign that touted, "Are you better off than you were four years ago?" Not many were better off than they were four years earlier, and they answered the question at the ballot box. Reagan won big.

Of course there were other reasons for Carter's defeat, not the least of which was the Iran hostage crises, but the economy was without a doubt the principal cause. Reagan found the weakest point in Carter's administration and pounded on it until it collapsed.

Also, big oil played a big role. The industry is loyal to nobody or no country. Even American oil companies wring every dollar out of a public helpless to counter their moves. We need oil to move people, to move goods and to move services. Almost no product goes unaffected by the price of oil

And yet, we subsidize them through our elected government. Check closely, and you will find a trail of campaign contributions to every candidate from either party for every office in the federal stream. Then they divert our attention.

Reagan's economic theory proposed the same thing Republican politicians had been brandishing in campaigns for several decades

—- balance the budget. Eight years of Reaganomics, however, produced not one balanced budget.

In fact, not only did the Reagan Administration fail to balance the budget, it produced year after year record breaking deficits, thus, together with his successor George Bush, increasing the five hundred ninety billion dollar national debt left him by Carter to four trillion dollars.

One must bear in mind that the national debt, though worrisome to many economists grew at such a slow pace from 1945 to 1975 that there was little concern in government circles and even less among those of us on the bottom. But the eighties saw an increase that was so geometrically compounded as to approach a vertical line on a graph of the growth trends of our debt. Reagan triple the national debt. George H. W. Bush double that again.

A good deal of the growth can be traced to the high interest rates of the late seventies and the early eighties, but the bulk of the blame goes on the "easy road" management mentality of the Congress and the Administrations we have had constructing our federal budgets. It seems everyone in both parties likes to talk about tax cuts, but nobody wants to raise taxes to pay for programs.

What nobody wants to admit is there is no such thing as a tax cut, when there is a deficit. There is only a tax shift. They shift it to a future generation. Somebody will someday have to pay it. But the generation receiving the services is not paying for them. For future generations, that is true taxation without representation. Who speaks for them?

We all know it takes a good measure of horse trading to reach agreement among five hundred and thirty-six politicians, which are our President and Congress, but it appears that in recent decades they have taken to trading away our future for their own.

The federal budget is a mere pork barrel to be used to buy future elections for members of this exclusive club we call Congress. One member takes home a new federal office building, another a new highway or bridge, still another gets new lands for a national park.

The result is new jobs in some districts or a new source of pride or tourist spending in another.

And even though the Congress supposedly did away with pork barrel spending, it still goes on. They just call it something else. More smoke and mirrors.

Everyone surmises that "this" district or State deserves it because all the others got something, and "why should we be left out?" So we each re-elect our representative because of the fine job of making sure we got our piece of the pie.

Never mind that together with all the members of Congress, due to such self-preserving, self-serving indulgences, we have exacerbated an already painful national financial malady, and we are merely passing it on to our children and grandchildren.

Decades ago our parents and their representatives did this same thing to us. At some point some generation is going to have to pay for this foolishness. Someone will have to pay in money or in pain; the kind of financial pain that plagued a generation in the 1930's. We got a taste of that future a few years ago. Did anybody learn anything?

This generation of Americans continues to hear promises of fiscal responsibility from the political establishment. Every year or so we hear the same old song carried by the hot air coming across the Potomac. Usually it comes in the form of pledges to reduce the deficit.

Note that there is no promise to balance the budget and eventually pay down and pay off the national debt, just to "reduce the deficit." This is a little like the "Guarantee" that comes with a used car, noted more for what is not covered than what is covered. An even better comparison is to the so called "sales" one sees from time to time in stores that are less than reputable.

How often have we read in an ad, "30% Off" or something like it? Off what? Many times the store that normally sold an item for seventy dollars would mark it up to one hundred. Then when the thirty percent discount was applied, it would sell for seventy dollars to "smart" shoppers who waited for the "sale".

This is the same computation process used to trim the deficit. If this year's deficit is three hundred billion dollars, we simply assume that next year it will be four hundred billion dollars. Then we tell the public that we are trimming 25% of the next fiscal year budget, leaving a deficit of "only" three hundred billion. That is Washington-speak.

To the rest of the human race (outside politics) reducing the deficit would be more like reducing a three hundred billion dollar deficit to two hundred fifty next year, two hundred the following year, one hundred the third year, maybe fifty billion dollars the fourth year and no deficit at all the fifth year, that is, a balanced budget.

Thereafter, a normal person might expect the government to begin to pay off, even in some small measures at first, the national debt. Of course, we are talking about normal people, who must handle their own finances, even in times of crisis, according to the rules of sound fiscal management. They cannot borrow from their grandchildren to secure their own present standing. Washington, on the other hand, borrows from everyone's grandchildren. And without anyone's permission.

On top of that, Congress reduces its revenues through tax cuts. What sane person would go into the bosses office and say, "Please reduce my income; I am trying to economize."? That is what a tax cut really does. If anything, they should increase taxes to at least the amount necessary to pay for what we are receiving, that is balance the budget.

And with debt comes interest. Interest is not one of the larger items in the federal budget, but it has been, and it will be again when rates go up. Money that might have built new bridges and highways; money that might have helped our schools; money that might have helped create our national health care program sooner or better; money that might have helped the poor leave public assistance and find good jobs; money that might have made our criminal justice system more effective and our lives more secure; money that might have lowered our taxes; money that must be used to pay for the "free lunch" of the eighties, the frantic spending of the seventies, the kind-hearted war on poverty of the sixties and the Cold War preparations of forty years.

The bill has come due. We must either continue to refinance it and will it to our children, or we must bite the bullet and start to pay it off. At some point we must face the economic realities.

Let's pause for a moment to reflect once more on the lessons of the 2008 economic collapse. Although it was worldwide, we have emerged much more quickly than other nations. Why?

For all the complaints and attacks on the Obama and Bush Administrations for their actions to abate the crisis, what they did worked. Obama especially has been criticized for bailing out the banks and GM. It is not a question of whether they deserved it. We as a nation had to avert a complete devastation of our economy.

The Administration and the Congress did what needed to be done. It was not pleasant, and it wasn't the best thing for us. But it was about the only thing we could do. And it worked. Our job creation has almost recovered completely; the stock market has reached historic levels; unemployment is half what it was at its worst; economic indicators are all optimistic. We can now address other issues, like the deficit and the debt.

This debt and its incessant growth are a cancer on our economy. Every dollar the government borrows is a dollar unavailable for business to use for growth, for home buyers, for auto buyers or for a host of other potential borrowers, who will use the money to stimulate the economy for the good of all. Instead our government uses it for the least good for us and the most good usually for themselves and their political fortunes.

The debt must be paid, or, at least for now, not increased. Labor unions must begin to learn from their mistakes. And we must grow the unions. They gave us the eight hour day, the weekend, vacations, sick leave, health coverage and so much more. They must begin to bargain for more than present earnings. Management must return to "patriotic profit".

These are the things that will return us to the leadership of the economic world in growth as well as size of economic market. Those behind us in size will catch us if we do not grow. Labor and management, consumer and producer, all must share this task. And the government must lead.

Those of us on the bottom are worried. We have watched unions bargain in the fifties and sixties for more pay and benefits, but not for secured retirement funds. There were no demands in the industrial East and Midwest for new modern manufacturing facilities or newer high technology equipment. We saw the old companies abandon the old inefficient buildings and the deteriorating old out-of-date machinery to move to new facilities and new equipment in new locations.

We witnessed the communities they left suffering the unemployment of long faithful employees, the deterioration of neighborhoods and schools, the growth of crime, and the lack of services. It was the management of the industries that made the decision to leave these "cradles" of the Industrial Revolution, but it was also the unions that allowed it to happen when they did not bargain for job security.

We on the bottom saw the industries leaving our towns for other new towns in other parts of the country, and in our dismay of the losses, failed to note that many were leaving not only our communities, but our country as well. They had determined that they could not be competitive without cheaper labor markets, without less-restrictive government controls and without better tax climates.

And yet, they still wanted the American flag for protection from tyrants and tariffs and weather and war. The American consumer is a valued customer, but not a valued employee. Perhaps such arrogance is justified by the foolishness of American buyers who continue to purchase products from companies that long ago deserted their homeland in time of global economic war. Some hesitate to call trade economic war, but there is no other word for what could cost us our economic freedom.

Unless labor and management quit fighting each other and turn instead to fight side by side for the preservation of our own economic well-being we could someday slide to third rate status in a world where everyone else is fighting to win.

Unless our government stops spending our money on government before we make it, we will continue to slide from recession to recession without noticeable gain in wealth among the nations of the world.

Already the disparity between the wealthy and the rest of us has grown practically enough to eliminate the middle class. Where once CEO's made twenty to forty times the average income of their workers, now it is common to find them making four or five hundred times the average worker's pay.

There is today a belief in the global market as an all-encompassing reality. Some would have us believe that our own fiscal status is secondary to that global market. We on the bottom do not live in a global community. We live in our families and in our communities first.

We rely on our States and our United States of America to secure the "blessings of liberty to ourselves and our posterity." The local market is the one that employs us, pays for our community services, educates our children and feeds our families.

When the global market is even and equal, when all workers are paid the same scale for the same jobs, when all nations give the same protection to our global environment, when all tax districts offer the same services and protections for the same rates, and when all humans on this earth have the same opportunities and responsibilities as we in America, then we can view a global market through the same eyes that see our local market.

Until then we expect the American government, American industry and American labor to protect our American jobs, families and communities. After all, we on the bottom ARE the American economy.

CLOWNS AND GLADIATORS

Fame is proof that the people are gullible.

Ralph Waldo Emerson (1803-1882)

The fame of a great man ought always to be estimated by the means used to acquire it.

Francois, Duc de la Rochefoucauld (1613-1680)

French writer and moralist

A case could be made that a people should be judged by its own values, that is, by the institutions it values most and the individuals it most admires. On the surface, then, America would rate well. After all, our Constitution, our long well known reverence for freedom and equality, and our emphasis on the sacredness of the individual in our society would seem to indicate a strong and well grounded sense of values.

But we should note that, in practice, we do not "put our money where our mouth is". If we did, the best paying jobs in America would be in areas of law enforcement, education, health care and personal services of all kinds. Our heroes would be great teachers, charity workers, life savers and others who showed us the best in human character. We all know those are not the American heroes of today.

Let's take a close look at the people admired most by Americans, and who most influence Americans. In general, those on the bottom, when pressed, will admit that it is those who make the least sacrifice to help others out of their own resources or would-be gain that seem to receive the most adoration, respect and money in today's America. It is usually those who entertain us, amuse us or inform us in an entertaining manner, that reap the greatest rewards. It is the entertainers, the athletes and electronic journalists (and talk show hosts) who are getting our attention, our loyalty and our money. The ancient fools, jesters, gladiators and messengers have come a long way.

Born of a revolt against a monarchy and its tyrannical government, the United States has from the beginning lacked mystique of royalty and nobility so common to the histories of the European nations who found these shores and settled this land. The colonists hated the overbearing and snobbish attitudes of the rulers and their governments in England, and the nobility of England tended to find no human value in the people who inhabited the colonies. They were merely a source of revenue to the mother country. Though it would take more than a hundred years for the influence of the nobility in Europe to die, it had in fact already begun to decline in importance, due to the growing intolerance among the people for the extravagances among nobles.

The founders of our democracy in their desire to keep what was good and discard the bad in the English system of government, established our Congress and Presidency to be similar to, but at the same time decidedly different from, the system in our mother country.

The President would be elected to a specific term of office, thus making the officeholder accountable to the voters and limit the time in office to that desired by the people. The Congress too was to be elected just as the English House of Commons, but with more power to balance against that of the President. The biggest change was in the upper house of the legislature, the Senate. Unlike the House of Lords, at that time the more powerful of the two chambers of Parliament, the members of the Senate would represent not a noble class, but the States, and they would serve not for life, but a set term of office.

Thus was the United States denied the pomp and glory of a royal house and its attending nobility. The early Americans did not miss them. In fact, they seemed to relish their absence. Later generations, however, came to regard their European cousins with monarchies differently, sometimes even enviously, especially in the twentieth century. And we continue that fascination in this century.

Our curiosity and outright nosiness in everything royal around the world but most especially in England has grown almost to the stage of what might easily be called a social adoption. We follow all the gossip and scandals as well as the majesty of the British Royal House as if Elizabeth II were our own queen. Note how we lavish affection on Prince William and Kate Middleton and their children, Prince George and new baby Charlotte.

But, alas, we have no real monarch, and the closest we come to any royalty is the way of life provided by our elected representatives in the Congress for themselves. They certainly claim royal treatment.

As for a nobility, we the people have created our own. It is not really a peerage, as such, with its automatic passing from one generation to another, although that has been tried from time to time, but it is a group of individuals elevated to lofty position on bases unrelated to traits which might merit such high place.

Such need have we for a class that we can admire and whose leadership we can hail, and so low have become our values on which we might base such admiration, that we have exalted many who are not worthy of such homage and are not capable of responsible leadership. The most logical choices for such calling would be of course the thinkers, the compassionate and those truly committed to betterment of humankind. These would probably make life better for all Americans and, by extension, all the world.

But Americans do not bestow their greatest favor like the Roman Church creates Cardinals or like big business seeks top managers.

We appreciate intellects and their contributions to better living. We applaud the Mother Theresas of the world for caring about people. Those who dedicate themselves to making life better for all receive only praise from the average American. We honor and cherish all who have the talents, abilities and commitment to raise human existence to ever higher levels.

Our greatest admiration, however, is reserved not for these with the most to give, but for those who take the most. We lavish our affections on the actors, the athletes and the famous journalists of our time, while practically ignoring the scientists, the healers, the educators and all who endeavor to better our society. It seems we value most as a society those who entertain and divert us. This must be a modern phenomenon. Never before in history were the clowns, the gladiators and the messengers so adored.

In ancient times and even in the middle ages, actors and jesters were usually slaves or serfs useful for very little other than to entertain the affluent, the upper classes. Families had little regard for a member who decided to commit to a life of entertaining others, as it was thought to be a low calling.

In others words, it produced nothing of value. There was certainly some real value in that actors produced incentive for playwrights to continue to create and other writers to write the great works we enjoy even today. Without the actors, we in all likelihood would not now have the works of Shakespeare, Milton, and hundreds of other great writers.

And the humor provided by the jesters and clowns must have alleviated what seems to have been an otherwise depressing existence for all, though their entertainment reached only a privileged few. They were, nevertheless, given no great measure of respect by their employers, little regard by the general populace and no appreciation by even their own families. Entertainers, in short, having seemingly little useful talent were kept like toys for amusement.

Athletes, like actors and jesters, historically have been used principally for entertainment. The Greeks of old have always been known to enjoy athletic competition, hence the ancient Olympic games. The Romans, having more blood-thirsty tastes, tended to divert themselves with gladiators fighting each other or wild animals.

The gladiators most often were captured slaves trained to fight in the Roman style in the arena for the entertainment of the general population. When one fought well, he was showered with wreaths and the affection of the audience. This was usually the lot of the victor, while that of the vanquished was at the whim of the crowd usually a gruesome death.

Even a victor on another day probably would find himself the loser in another contest, and the ultimate end of almost all gladiators was death in the arena, though some very few were spared by some sponsor, who as a member of the elite could have a particular slave elevated to the rank of citizen. Still the plight of those who were less than "citizens" was determined by their status as beings useless except for amusement.

It was not until the modern era that athletes began to achieve recognition for their prowess and their sports. The advent of the modern Olympic Games brought with them renewed interest in athletic competition, but this time not just for the amusement of the spectators. The crowds were still important, however, they were needed mostly to encourage the competitors, not to determine any outcome of the events.

The true value of the Olympic Games is in their peaceful competition among nations of the world. Through them the youth of the world "fight" each other for supremacy in various events without the extremely debilitating effects of war. War still exists today, unfortunately, but perhaps someday the harmless competition of the Olympics can replace the brutal ambition which is in every case the seed of war. The Olympics are not a necessity, but they are useful; they lack great influence in the world as yet, but they are entertaining.

139

One of the principal events in the modern Olympics is the marathon, a contest that developed from a historical attempt to send a message in battle. The messenger ran for approximately twenty-six miles to deliver a message that ultimately brought victory. The race is a modern celebration of the success of that early message run.

It must be noted that there is little said about the messenger, who was apparently unimportant, as were all messengers throughout history. The only one ever to be given any recognition in all of history was Paul Revere, whose "The British are coming" is learned by every school student in America. Aside from Revere, however, messengers have historically been anonymous. The message was important, not the carrier. In fact, quite often messengers have been beaten or killed because the messages they brought were bad news.

Messengers generally were chosen from the ranks of the least useful in society, whether military or civilian. Good soldiers were kept for the battle; those less capable used for messengers. Other than Paul Revere, there are no accounts of famous messengers. No great leaders have come up from their ranks.

In early America, the town crier was important for keeping the townsfolk informed, but there are no common accounts of any crier who rose to become President, or Member of Congress, or Governor, or Mayor or business leader or any other kind of leader. After all, the town crier was not delivering information that he himself created, discovered or made. He was simply passing what was imparted to him, much as the telegraph and later the telephone accomplished mechanically.

The messenger was more of a medium than a person, and although not considered as low on the social ladder as actors and athletes, messengers were not a group parents wanted their children to grow up to join.

Certainly newspaper owners were persons of influence in the community, but their journalists did not achieve prominence as professionals until the time of the Civil War and beyond. Even then relatively few became well known, and their compensation was never until today competitive with other crafts.

Those on the bottom in the United States still must read or hear the messengers with a healthy skepticism. It is no secret that many or even most journalists report from their own slanted viewpoint, and may not present pure information on any given subject or event. That is precisely because today messengers are not confined to just delivering the messages.

They now have a hand in forming the message. This is a total departure from the historical role of the messenger. Today's messenger, like today's actor and today's athlete, is unlike any historical predecessors. This is true of all three in how they practice their crafts, how they view themselves in society and, most importantly, how they are viewed by society.

Today they are all entertainers in some way, even the journalists, the purveyors of information. It is the way modern America operates that requires everything destined for the consumer be packaged in the most enjoyable form. One of the goals of actors is entertainment. A secondary goal of athletic competition is the entertainment of the observers. Now even information must be entertaining, whether in directions on a map or highway, instructions for assembling many devices, or in the schools.

Natural social evolution has now brought us journalists who must be entertaining. Newspapers have new "more enjoyable" formats, and, of course, TV news personalities have had to adapt to more enjoyable delivery or see the TV scrap pile.

This is most evident in the cases of television news anchors, both male and female. They must be solid journalists today with extensive experience; but in addition they have to be attractive, witty and "entertaining".

News staffs constantly seem to be reorganizing to achieve the right combination of news anchors and weather and sports reporters in local markets, and the major national networks are in intense competition to attract the sizable audience necessary to bring the highest advertising revenues. Television news is, after all, first a business.

This business aspect of information delivery today has created a new class of highly recognizable, attractive, trusted and famous news reporters. The major television news personalities are so well known and so well trusted that few would doubt that any one of them might easily be elected to high public office.

Walter Cronkite was touted only a few years ago as a possible candidate for everything from Governor to U.S. Senator to President. More recently there was talk of NBC's Tom Brokaw running for the U.S. Senate when he tired of his anchor seat. Instead, he does special projects for the network, and he writes. Others have been mentioned, and still others, in mostly local markets, have run for public office and won.

It is no wonder that some of such notoriety can command such support from voters who routinely and trustingly look to them to keep them informed on the major issues of the day. Small wonder, indeed, that people would trust the messenger as if the creator of the message, since viewers come to regard TV journalists they see every day almost as trusted friends.

Americans feel as though they know these journalists personally. The same can be said for many actors and athletes. Familiarity among large groups of fans certainly helped former Buffalo Bills quarterback Jack Kemp and former New Jersey Nets player Bill Bradley to be elected to represent Buffalo and New Jersey respectively in the U.S. House of Representatives and the U.S. Senate.

And being seen every week by millions, including folks back home in Iowa had to give an election campaign advantage to U.S. Representative Fred Grande, a regular on the seventies television series THE LOVE BOAT.

Movie actor George Murphy rode his fame to the U.S. Senate, and Ronald Reagan's admirers and critics alike know that the greatest role he ever played was President of the United States.

Clint Eastwood and Sonny Bono are also on the list of famous personalities who have gone on to or paused for service in public office. Others have authored best-selling books on subjects or issues that have caught the public eye. Moreover, the influence of famous personalities extends beyond those who hold or seek public office themselves.

It is remarkable to many of us on the bottom how such large numbers of the people in some quarters seem susceptible to the influence and opinions of personalities who are no better informed or educated on the issues than the average person.

Nevertheless, it must work. Since John F. Kennedy and before him Truman and Eisenhower, Presidential candidates have trotted out the likes of Sammie Davis Jr., Frank Sinatra, Charlton Heston, Bob Hope, Barbra Streisand and a host of other well liked entertainment personalities to help win votes.

Congressional and state office candidates also make frequent use of supportive performers. Even local candidates will use well known local TV and radio personalities to help their candidacies. Sometimes they can make a crucial difference by bringing an extra few votes to help a candidate to victory.

It doesn't say much for the way our modern democracy works. It is a true indictment of our society that we bestow such importance on the opinions of individuals simply because of their fame or notoriety and not because of any well-schooled understanding of the issues at hand.

The same is true of the journalists and the so-called journalists, the latter being the modern day gossipmongers we call talk show hosts. These are to many the worst sources of serious information. Although they often present serious topics, they just as often pervert the presentation to prevent adequate enlightenment for the viewer or listener.

Whether the host is Rachel Ray, Ellen DeGeneres, the various late night hosts or any number of others, the general trend of each show is to present some person or persons in some very abnormal or controversial situation and then allow the audience with the help of the host either to support the guests or degrade them in way reminiscent of the Roman gladiator spectacles. One might easily imagine the lions eating the Christians.

The subjects of the programs seem to mirror those found in publications bought near the checkout counter in most grocery stores and supermarkets. What is really being sold by the sponsors of this quasi-trash is sensationalism and titillation.

Of course there are better and worse ones. Oprah Winfrey appears to have a program driven more by her pleasant personality than by risque topics, although from time to time she too has some of questionable merit. And she has "spin-offs" in Dr. Phil and Dr. Oz.

The hosts of these shows, of course, defend them as educational in every way, providing valuable information to an under-informed public. The doctors, especially, purport to be bringing valuable information to the public.

There has been a proliferation of these programs over the last several decades. They are cheap to produce and lucrative in advertising revenues. Jerry Springer has made a fortune exploiting the "Barnum and Bailey" crowd among TV viewers.

On the more respectable side, we used to have shows like Ted Koppel's Nightline and Larry King Live, along with various news magazine shows like 60 Minutes and 20/20. These were more informative and were more like regular magazines such as Time and Newsweek, except for the limits of content due to time limitations. But, now Koppel and King are retired, and there was nobody of that caliber to replace them.

Some topics are blown up to give them greater importance than they deserve, and some are not given the supportive research they may deserve, but the greatest criticism must be given to practice, especially common on interview type shows, of having expert guests who debate with other experts and are never asked questions the average viewer wants answered.

The view from the bottom is so misunderstood even by the best interviewers that these questions are not obvious to them, nor are the opinions of the average American. That is the reason for this book in the first place, that is, to try to give some small indication of the unimportant (to the high placed) opinions of those of us on the bottom in America.

Some of these opinions are heard occasionally on Talk Radio. Prime examples of today's radio talk show hosts are Howard Stern (possibly the worst in terms of taste and judgement) and Rush Limbaugh (not the best, but at least tolerable).

Stern seems bent on lowering the standards of acceptable human behavior to its lowest possible point. Most of his talk and his subjects are unnecessary and uninformative. He appears to be a mere outlet for pent up anxiety and hostility among the less productive in our society. Few Phi Beta Kappa's, it would seem, would have reason to listen to his ravings. Ultimately, legitimate radio, if there is such a thing, relegated him to satellite broadcasting.

Limbaugh, a political caricature of a television evangelist, preaches daily on behalf of his first love, the Republican Party. There is nothing wrong with his devotion to the party, but he should be honest enough not to hold himself and his program up to the public as a forum. He is not there to promote debate, analysis, compromise or even-handed discussion.

His goal is similar to that of a campaign ad —- to elect his party's candidate. The goal is not evil, but why not be honest and say so? He might even be reminded that the 1992 Presidential election is over. Bill Clinton won. Limbaugh was critical of everything that administration did since the first burp after the inaugural dinner. It is safe to assume that even the new wallpaper in the White House bathrooms was not to his liking. And now that Hillary Clinton has chosen to seek the White House, Limbaugh has dusted off all his old Clinton ammo.

Vitriol flows easily from him. Praise must be reserved for the next Republican President (although George W. Bush failed to measure up to Rush's 'conservative' expectations), assuming there is one during Limbaugh's remaining lifetime. I don't recall ever hearing him agree with or praise even ONE policy of the Obama Administration.

Loyalty to one's country, it would seem, should transcend loyalty to any particular political philosophy or party. Limbaugh's loyalty to the Republican Party is exceeded or at least matched by his devotion to wealth and himself. The most notable item in the set of his television show is the profligate display of the dozens of copies of his books, an easy subliminal ad.

Sean Hannity is another mud-slinger. He constantly assaults anyone to his left. With his views, Attila the Hun might not pass muster. He searches for negatives on any Democrat or less-than-far-right-wing Republican. If he can't find any, he makes them up.

FoxNews, a misleading label, purports to present news in a balanced fashion, but everyone seems to be ultra right wing, except for a few moderate tokens. Most often, they present the Republican slant on all issues. This is to offer balance, they say, to CNN and MSNBC, who they say are in the pockets of the liberals. To be sure, there is a liberal slant to the news at those networks, but not nearly to the extent the right is represented by Fox.

The public in America has encouraged such money-grabbing efforts by its ostensible approval of blatant over-compensation of entertainers, be they performers, journalists or athletes. The American consumer is numb to the constant rain of good fortune on these "Most Valued Players" in the game of modern life.

Today it is quite common for Football players in the National Football League to sign contracts assuring them of fifteen, twenty, even thirty million dollars over several years. Major League baseball players can earn five or six million a year; National Basketball Association players can earn eight or ten million a year.

The national television networks routinely pay millions to their news anchors. It is no secret that actors have been making millions for many years, at least, the big stars do. It is not uncommon for a major actor to command tens of millions for a film. Average working people in the United States used to gasp in unbelief at such news, but today it is so common as to be almost not newsworthy. We should all be appalled.

Many of these celebrities have for years defended such exorbitant compensation, on the grounds that their careers may be limited to a few short years (athletes) or the law of supply and demand for quality entertainment (actors) or the long climb to the top (journalists). Nonsense! Athletes are playing a game.

It should not even be a career. A career is a vocation providing serious service to others through comprehensive training and education and hard work. Most athletes are adults playing children's games, and they are entertaining an audience.

The part that commands the money is the entertainment, televised entertainment, that draws advertisers and their money. And the jealous resentment of the public takes the form of mere grumbling, short-lived grumbling at that. That the American public condones this absurdity by continuing to buy the products of the advertisers and by continuing to attend the games is a testament to the values of our society.

Who are the highest paid groups in America? The workers who produce all the time- and labor-saving devices we depend on today? No! The teachers who educate our children to give them an opportunity to compete in highly technical fields of the future? No! The public servants who provide the services that keep our communities, our States and our nation operating? No! The health care professionals who keep our health and often save our lives? No, even though we complain, sometimes justifiable, of their high pay.

No, it is none of these or a myriad of others who provide real services and products to make life tolerable if not indeed better. The highest paid are the entertainers, those people who are paid to amuse us, to divert us, to take our minds off the serious and minor problems of life for a little while.

This diversion is no unimportant facet of modern American life. We live such a complex existence today, that it is essential for us to "get away from it all" for at least part of the time. There is both relief from problems and anxieties and a variety added to our lives that reduces the negative impact that the pressures of Twenty-first Century American life exert on us.

Notwithstanding the positive and even necessary catharsis provided to us by entertainers, their relative merits alongside those of educators, healers and many others in our society make their inordinate and unnecessary compensation seem obscene. Through ordinary and even reasonably extravagant living, nobody is going to spend what some of them make in a lifetime, or even through several generations.

And why should some inherit the right not to have to work, not to have to learn, not to have to be productive in any sense, especially when that inheritance was for questionable work value.

Others who work hard and provide valuable services or products are quite often undercompensated. The America tamed by pioneers who endured hardship for the sake of opportunity would certainly be ashamed of an America in which opportunity has been replaced by opportunism.

And as for the influence of the famous on the workings of our society, whether they be using their celebrity status to sell the consumer soap or an automobile or a candidate, it is the gullible public that grants them the special status they hold.

When the public awakens to its own needs and its own real value, the door will be shut on such outrageous abuse of trust, and perhaps then the clowns and the gladiators and the messengers will return to providing the services they do well for the compensation that reflects their relative value to society, just as the rest of us must do in the best of all worlds. And maybe then the recommendation of the plumber or the teacher or the nurse or the auto worker will sell just as much soap or just as many cars.

AND JUSTICE FOR ALL

Who thinks the law has anything to do with justice? It's what we have because we can't have justice.

William McIlvanney (b. 1836)

British Novelist

From the pure ideal of our founding fathers, our justice system has devolved from a system attempting to balance the wants and needs of every person so that none might prevail over another, to one that protects the rights of a violator over those of a victim. It provides for those who would use it to overcompensate one for a loss at the expense of not only the person who caused the loss, but the whole of society as well.

Our courts have taken such liberty in interpreting the Constitution so as to legislate from the bench. Thus, it is cruel and unusual punishment to provide incarceration for criminals that equals the facilities we provide for military personnel who volunteer to defend our country, or the poor who depend on public assistance to survive.

It has become a system which encourages litigation to resolve all differences, and protects and encourages the vile in our society who prey upon the weak. We on the bottom know what has caused this calamity. We have watched it grow. We want it changed, and we know who can change it and how it should be changed. We hope our democratic system will hear us.

In a democratic society where liberty and equality are, in absolute form, the ultimate goal for all as a people, real justice is the only way to achieve that goal. Unfortunately, justice seems such an elusive creature, ever sought, but never caught. Throughout our history as a nation we have been reminded over and over that we are a nation of laws, not of men.

That fact more than anything else has made us the success we are as a nation. We have avoided the turmoil that has existed in most countries in the world, where personalities determine the government either in form or policy.

Monarchies and empires are obvious in this regard, but many democracies have had difficulties retaining stable government structures or policies because of fluctuating loyalties of large segments of their populations to various political personalities. Parliamentary democracies are somewhat more susceptible to such instability, since a government can fall on a vote of confidence.

France after World War II suffered a succession of weak ineffective governments that fell one after the other, until DeGaulle founded the Fifth Republic, which, like the U.S., has a strong president to balance the parliament.

Italy is the best example today of the instability of government dependent on personalities more than the law itself. Approximately fifty governments in the last fifty years have proven incapable of conducting stable domestic and foreign policy in a country that has given so much of what is now modern European culture and civilization. And this doesn't even include the problems with audacious corruption.

In the United States, by contrast, our system has survived the volatile personalities of several presidents and numerous members of the Congress, as well as some dubious characters who have sat on the Supreme Court. Moreover, we have endured Civil War and Depression, both of which threatened our very existence as a nation.

Add to these the various wars and social upheavals we have seen, including the dissident movements in the 1960's, together with the civil rights movement and the anti-war activities during the

Vietnam War, and this social experiment we call the United States of America has proven to be extremely resilient.

Straying into wars around the globe over dubious U.S. national interests, the extreme partisanship of both houses of Congress and the strange actions of state governments across the nation have shaken the confidence of the public in the ability of our government to actually govern. And even the courts have given new cause for concern.

Supreme Court rulings on civil rights and election financing have brought doubts about the safety of our process and institutions. Efforts to curtail voting among minorities and other segments of society, together with rulings allowing unlimited and unidentified monies to play an ever increasing role in our election campaigns would seem to limit our ability to elect the real choices of the people. And yet we are not without hope.

Why? Because personalities, some great and some not so great, have come and gone, but we have survived by rule of law. We have allowed our lawmakers and law enforcers to take the actions necessary to hold us together. We have accepted as a people that they are acting within the authority we have given them.

But laws, accepted and enforced as they may be, do not guarantee justice. They are merely guideposts on the road to justice, and the road is neither straight nor short. It is a rough road with many detours and many pitfalls. The signs along the way are often misleading and even more often wrong.

Laws are made to address specific issues or problems; they prevent chaos; they soothe painful injuries; they attempt to right certain wrongs. But they do not necessarily yield justice. In essence laws are made to provide, and to keep, order. Thus, the phrase "law and order" seems to be used almost as a single word in America, especially by politicians.

Order, though, is much more difficult to maintain in a society where freedom is the by-word. In fact, the words "freedom" and "order" by definition and function seem to be at odds with one another. Can they really exist in pure form side by side? Some might justifiably question such a notion.

However, we in America seem to have reached at least some balance between the two. When that balance is upset, our social health is jeopardized. When the laws fail to address or solve a problem, or when lawmakers fail to make a necessary law, or when the law enforcers seem unable to enforce a law adequately, society begins to lose faith in the law and in the system.

Our system with all its flexibility and all its resilience has several problems today which, if allowed to continue unchecked and unchanged, will challenge our ability as a people to maintain our freedom and our good order.

One of the greatest problems we must face is the litigious nature of contemporary American society. It seems that every injury, every loss, every slight, no matter how small, must be settled in court. Everyone wants compensation for every offense. Everyone wants punitive damages from every offender.

The questions we should be asking are, "Who should determine punitive damages?", "How much is punitive?", "What justifies punitive damages?", Who really pays punitive damages?" and "What are the real costs?" But before we try to answer any of these, we must decide if it is healthy to allow indiscriminate lawsuits to be filed for every notion under the sun.

There are lawsuits filed every day in every part of this country that are groundless, and the plaintiffs and their lawyers know they are groundless. Some are filed as a strategy to encourage the other party to settle the issue or issues which have antagonized them. Some are frivolous, but the frivolity is not provable.

It was once estimated that forty percent of the lawsuits filed in the courts of Nevada were filed by inmates. Some are certainly warranted due to some real violation of civil or legal rights, but it is safe to assume that a great many, and probably a majority, are merely an intriguing game played by the inmates to avoid boredom or avenge themselves against the system that has incarcerated them. This goes on in every state in the union.

A person injured in an auto accident or at work sues to recover damages for medical costs, loss or earnings during disability, loss of property, loss of family time, pain and suffering and anything else that can be described as a loss. Most are easily justified. No person should suffer financial loss because of the negligent acts of others, but how can a price be placed on loss of family time or pain and suffering? Furthermore, what amount of compensation can alleviate such loss?

Surely, some amount might be awarded as a token, but, unfortunately, in our system, this is not decided pragmatically. We ask a jury made up of our peers, that is, average people prone to emotion, to decide based on their emotional response to the facts presented how much money to award to an injured person. Emotion, especially sympathy for the victim and outrage at the offender, often brings a large award. In some cases these awards can be in the millions of dollars.

And who gets these millions? A victim who can use the money to try to piece back together a comfortable life? No! Quite often the money will be banked to provide interest to help with daily expenses, and then passed on at death to survivors who did not suffer any pain and suffering and whose losses of family time will be forgotten while spending the deceased relative's unused and un-enjoyed fortune.

Meanwhile the jurors who awarded this "judicial lottery" prize probably went home and complained about their next insurance premium increase, or their next doctor or medical expense or the taxes that went up on them, never realizing they helped make it all possible. These and others are the true costs of such an unreliable system of compensating victims.

A great bit of our insurance dollars are to cover expenses paid by insurance companies due to punitive damages. Actual damages to property or bodily injury are rarely as much, since they are based on verifiable information. And what about the cost to taxpayers of the extra court personnel and facilities to attend to all the law suits.

In addition, just about every item or service we buy has built into the price some amount to pay for insurance coverage for the manufacturing or servicing or selling facility.

Doctors especially are hard hit when it comes to insurance, particularly malpractice insurance. Some are paying tens of thousands of dollars each year for the privilege of practicing medicine. That cost is passed on to everyone else in the form of higher fees.

Everyone in business pays for insurance. The hardware store, the restaurant, the plumber, the homebuilder, the mechanic, the auto dealer, the real estate broker, the public and private schools, government agencies, and even the insurance agent must have insurance to engage in their normal activities. They must pass the cost on as a cost of doing business. That means we all pay for our insurance and everyone else's, too.

It is readily apparent that too much of our finances as a people are going to pay for the results of our system of redress. Notice the word redress, not justice. There is great abuse of our civil laws, and it is costing too much. What can we do to improve the system?

For one thing we can remove punitive damage awards from the purview of juries and involve a judge with the advice of other experts in such an award. In most criminal cases, juries determine guilt, and judges within the parameters provided by law assign sentence or punishment.

In civil cases, as well, juries should determine guilt or liability, and judges with expert advice should assign the punitive damages. The advice might come from panels of experts on quality of life and financial matters. In any event juries should determine guilt or innocence; judges should pronounce penalties.

And punitive damages should be paid by the person causing the injury in question, not by an insurance company. There is no punishment, if someone else is paying for it. Just as a criminal cannot hire someone to serve a sentence, a civil defendant should not be able to "hire" an insurance company to pay the penalty. We all must begin to assume responsibility for our own actions.

Responsibility is not assigned specifically in the U.S. Constitution. Many rights are protected, but no responsibilities required. Again, we are a nation of laws, not justice.

One prime example of this is the case of a baby named Jessica. She was given up for adoption by her single mother. Later, when the biological father found out, he insisted on marrying the mother and taking back "his baby". Two and a half years of court battles won the biological parents the custody. Never mind that the adoptive couple and Jessica were now emotionally a family.

How can a two and a half year old child understand losing the only parents she knows? Justice was not done in the "Baby Jessica" case. Justice was not given to Jessica, nor to her adoptive parents nor to her biological parents, but the law was followed. It is doubtful her rights were considered, since they are not among those described in the Constitution. She was not denied freedom of speech, religion or press, nor any civil right mentioned.

She was denied a moral right, the right to grow up in a secure environment of love and responsibility. Instead, she was placed in one, where the right of parental ownership prevailed, where neither parent felt any obligation toward each other until the opportunity of ownership of a child developed. Their action in producing the baby was irresponsible and one of no apparent devotion to each other.

The mother's decision to give the baby for adoption was the one act of decency on the part of either of them. After that, their rights under the law became more important than any moral right of anyone else involved. The resulting injustice faults the law.

And how many others in our society today speak forcefully of their rights under the Constitution, with absolutely no thought of any responsibility they may have morally toward the other human beings with whom they share space in this country?

Parents let their children die without medical attention based on their right to freedom of religion. They thought God would heal their child. It never occurred to them that He sent the doctor and the pharmacist and others to do just that —- heal the child.

There are also those who practice hate under the banner of freedom of speech. That freedom gives them the right to cause untold pain to others without penalty. Freedom of the press gives tabloids the right to print outright lies, and it gives the so-called legitimate press the power of a fourth branch of government to wield influence for the few who control it in shaping our laws and our government.

A newspaper endorsement can give a political candidate a victory in a close race, and it never shows up on a campaign finance report. The value is unquestionable, but the newspaper never admits to being a contributor. They can do the same on any issue, but they are the first to complain about the so-called pay-to-play nature of the relationship between lobbyists and government.

And what about the billionaires, who can pay for numerous and forceful ads supporting or denigrating a candidate, thus determining the outcome of an election?

And then there is the right to bear arms. We have unquestionably the most violent society in the developed world. Each day one hundred thousand guns are carried to school by children. The leading cause of death to boys in the United States is gunshot, and that is among whites and non-whites.

Every day we read of some maniac shooting people down in restaurants with automatic weapons, or somebody shooting another to death in a courtroom or a crazy who shoots up an office staffed with co-workers.

We have an epidemic of domestic violence, spouses beating each other, especially men beating women, and parents beating children, sometimes to death.

Every year twenty-six thousand people die on our highways, many because of drunken drivers. We have people selling drugs to even our children, and organized crime flourishing in an international market. This is the global market at its worst. And most of the crime is perpetrated with or enforced by guns. And yet, there is a loud cry from many, particularly the National Rifle Association, at the mere mention of gun control.

The Second Amendment to the Constitution says that since a well armed militia is necessary to the defense of freedom, the right to bear arms shall not be abridged. We have a well armed militia. It is called the National Guard. And the right to bear arms is not abridged by requiring information to ensure that convicted felons, those with mental disabilities, children and others who should not have them can't get them.

No one needs a canon. No one needs a machine gun or a rocket launcher, unless a member of the military or a police force. The same may be said of hand guns. If no one had them but military or police personnel, we would all benefit.

They are useful only to kill or maim a human being. They are nearly useless for any type of hunting, as they are quite inaccurate from a distance. Yet, despite all the senseless killing, the NRA and their allies insist this right is inviolate. Nonsense!

In May 2015, there was a fight among rival motorcycle gangs in Waco, Texas. It spilled out into the parking lot of a shopping center. Nine were killed and eighteen wounded before the police could end the conflict. They arrested 170 and confiscated over one hundred weapons, including knives, clubs, brass knuckles and lots of guns. They found even more guns and rifles in the vehicles they impounded from those charged in the case. Such proliferation endangers everyone in the area.

The first right under the Constitution is the right to life. Inasmuch as guns interfere with that and the right to liberty and the pursuit of happiness, then, to the degree necessary, the right to bear arms must be limited. At the very least the Brady Bill has served that purpose.

We need more control to eliminate totally the instant access to hand guns with no period of time to check on the purchaser to insure that person is eligible to own such a weapon. Automatic weapons should be totally illegal in a civilized nation such as what we wish to be.

If we were to spread the liability for any illegal action involving a gun to the seller, the distributor and the manufacturer, perhaps they might join in the efforts to ensure responsible ownership.

In one area of this dispute the NRA is most certainly correct. Our law enforcement system is very ineffective when it comes to preventing violent crime. The civil rights of criminal defendants in this country in some ways exceed those of all others, especially victims.

If a person is shot to death, the weapon may be the prime evidence, but if an overzealous police officer obtains the weapon in an illegal search, it may be inadmissible as evidence and, thus, set a murderer free. This vicious criminal is freed, because another, the officer, violated another law. The victim's right to life is violated a second time. The grief of the family is intensified.

If justice were truly to be served, the murderer would still be punished, and the officer would be punished as well for a separate offense of violating the illegal search provisions of the law. To free the guilty in the face of absolute evidence is to compound the crime.

Part of the problem is the courts in the United States. Our courts have consistently interpreted the law to allow the greatest possible individual freedoms from responsibility. From negligible enforcement of parental support orders to granting parole and probation to violent felons to freeing the guilty through loopholes to lax sentencing, many judges today seem to be unaware of the damage they may unleash on the public.

An individual accused of violating deserves every protection the law can provide to insure a fair impartial trial based on true evidence.

Once found guilty beyond the shadow of a doubt, the convict deserves the full fair punishment of the law. To be sure, this is not always easy. Even after an unquestionably fair conviction, there are other considerations. One great one is the serious lack of prison space in most States.

How often we have heard of prison riots and other problems arising from the lack of prison space and the crammed conditions of the cells available. Court cases have even forced the release of some before their sentences are served and no prison time for others because of unavailability of room.

In addition we have prisoners suing over poor or nonexistent recreational facilities or educational programs or law libraries. Perhaps we pamper our prisoners too much, especially the violent ones.

These are not supposed to be rest homes or vacation camps. These prisoners are people who broke the law, many times hurting others in the process. They should be sentenced as in military courts to hard labor. Work should be required, and not just a forty hour week. Prisoners tired from work don't riot; they sleep. They might also have less time to plan escapes.

As to the cost of building more prisons, it might be more cost efficient to eliminate State prisons for violent felons. We might be better served by a federal prison system for such offenders, allowing the States to pay the actual cost per prisoner to incarcerate them.

The administrative cost savings would help, but the ability of the federal prison system to hold and control prisoners has a much better record than the States as a group. There have been few if any escapes or riots involving federal facilities. For the most threatening, why not build a prison in the Alaskan wilderness (this is not to suggest a Siberian-like Gulag)? No fences would be necessary. No one is going to hike a hundred miles through stretches of nothing but snow to escape.

Put a military camp next to it. The guards come with the camp. There can be plenty of work moving snow and stoking furnaces. Maybe there could be a greenhouse where the prisoners could cultivate their own food. And no prisoner will ever want to return. This prison is a must for drug dealers who are used to the climate found usually in the Caribbean and South America.

This brings us to the war on drugs. What a war! In a real war both sides inflict casualties on each other until one side cannot absorb any more. In this war most if not almost all of the casualties are on our side, and they are not even the fighters. They are the victims of the drug dealers. Sometimes they are drug dealers who are caught in the market wars that they fight among themselves.

The high command on the other side is living comfortably in South and Central American mansions, and some in European and North American mansions. At any rate, the war goes on, and our side is many times limited to a role of observer. A real war would plan assaults on the other side, not on the small camp, but on the headquarters, or at least command structures. Then they would inflict casualties. Our courts would back them up.

Our Navy and Coast Guard should have the authority to board suspected drug ships on the high seas. If the suspected cargo is found, there should follow a military trial at sea with appropriate execution of sentence. This is a real war. No one seems to want to believe that.

The other side has declared the war. They are fighting the war. They are inflicting casualties. They are killing our brothers and sisters and neighbors. And, worst of all, they are killing our children.

They are infesting and may ultimately destroy our society. That is real war. We must fight it like a real war. We must fight to win. If that means executing the traitors to our own side, then that is what we must do.

American drug dealers prey on the weak among us. They do it for money. They would destroy all that America is for money or drugs or both. A nation that could execute the Rosenbergs for selling secrets to the Soviets ought to be able to execute those who threaten to do even worse —- to kill our children.

Our solution to the drug problems seems to be to arrest and incarcerate the low level users and sellers. Our prisons are overcrowded with these average people caught up in the abuse and hooked. They were caught using or selling some to a friend. They possess very little of the drugs, but they are sent to prison. Most often they are minorities. Whites get better lawyers and are treated more leniently.

So the prisons are full of minor offenders, who could be dealt with more efficiently and successfully through social systems. Meanwhile, the generals and commanders among our enemies are insulated and immune in most cases.

But more recently, our allies in Central America have experienced more success in apprehending or killing some of the biggest cartel leaders. With our help, these efforts have increased and improved. More resources must be allocated to this fight. Some of the leaders have been killed or executed.

The question of capital punishment is one that comes to the public debate regularly, or maybe constantly. Those who oppose it do so in good conscience. There is a serious, valid argument that a person executed and subsequently found to be innocent cannot be restored to life, and there is done, therefore, an unrightable wrong.

This point cannot easily be dismissed. Any time there is even a remote possibility that a person convicted of a capital crime is innocent, then there must be an alternative sentence to hold that person until that uncertainty is eliminated. If that means a life sentence, it is preferable to the possibility of executing an innocent person.

But, if that is not a consideration, if there is no doubt, then society must be prepared to act swiftly in the execution of the sentence. If the death penalty is to have any effect, it must be swift and sure. The system of appeals in this country wherein a convicted killer can delay execution of sentence for ten, fifteen, even twenty years, dilutes the effect of the penalty.

That said, it should be noted, that the author is opposed to capital punishment on religious grounds. God put a mark on Cain and said, "Woe unto him who kills Cain." In other words, God reserves that right to Himself.

We should have an appellate system just for the death penalty, so that an appeal of a capital conviction might be heard expeditiously and a ruling made. Moreover, if further appeal is made to the Supreme Court, such a capital case should be moved to the front of the docket, so as to provide the earliest possible hearing.

A final ruling should be made as soon as possible, not to exact the blood payment in revenge, but to satisfy the right of all to speedy justice, and to serve as an example to others that blatant disregard for human life will not be tolerated in any way by a truly civilized society. To those who object to the death penalty as cruel and inhuman might be noted that to keep a person in a cage for twenty, thirty, forty or fifty years is hardly humane. This is not a matter of one being more humane than the other. It is a matter of punishment to fit the crime.

There is a legitimate argument to having true life imprisonment without parole. It is not objectionable to moralists, and it is certainly justifiable. There would be no execution of innocents, and the cost is considerably less than the cost of appeals in capital cases.

There have been sadistic monsters who have mutilated, tortured and killed in the most hideous ways. Even the death penalty as it is now executed in the United States cannot possibly offer punishment sufficient to balance against the weight of such a crime.

For one who could beat a child to death as some have, in such a flagrant disregard for any humane standard, the death penalty is hardly too harsh. For a killer who could kill in cold blood an elderly and weak person for money for drugs, the death penalty is the only answer to many. These are not people who can ever be rehabilitated, for they have no respect for life itself, for any human being, and, in most cases, for themselves. Nobody could question life without parole for those.

In 1982 in Mississippi, a man was executed for torturing, molesting and holding the face of a two-year-old girl in the mud until she was asphyxiated. There were many who said he was executed out of an emotional response. It can be argued that anyone who would not feel an emotional bent to revenge in such a case is hardly human, but one need only look at the prisoner's history to find the justification.

That same man had not long before been released from prison in Texas on parole after serving seven years for the murder of his seventeen-year-old girl friend. Instead of death, he was sentenced to serve prison time. Instead of serving his entire sentence, he was paroled.

Had he served his entire sentence, perhaps he would not have been in Mississippi to murder the child, or at least not until later, and maybe it might not have happened at all.

Some might argue had he been executed for the first murder, the little girl might still be alive today. She would be twenty-three. When the Texas parole board set the prisoner free, they sentenced that little girl to capital punishment for no crime at all.

Our penal system and our court system reflect our society as a whole. We are a permissive society. We are a people who do not like responsibility. We all want the right to do what we please, even though what we please may violate someone else's rights.

This selfish trend is born once again of the emergence of the Baby Boomer generation and its desire to have every want, every need and every inclination satisfied instantly and without cost. Our reservation of a right, legal or civil, for everything in life is an outgrowth of the pattern we began in the fifties.

The discipline of hard work and sacrifice that shaped a nation for two hundred years has been replaced by self-indulgence as individuals and as a nation. Our legal system only reflects what we are willing to demand of ourselves.

And the generations after the Baby Boomers are even worse in demanding even more "rights" and acknowledging fewer and fewer responsibilities.

If we are to mold our nation of laws into a nation of true justice, we must straighten the path, pave it into a highway, change the signs so that they direct us well and shorten the distance to our objective. It is said that justice delayed is justice denied. There are many and have been many more whose justice still waits.

Thomas Jefferson once said, "I trouble for my country when I reflect that God is just; that his justice cannot sleep forever." We as a country should heed his thought, for there is much for us to do before the pledge of allegiance to our flag can be a pledge to our children to bring them a society of "liberty and justice for all".

POLITICS IN AMERICA

Do Unto Others.......FIRST!

The tragedy of one successful politician after another is the gradual substitution of narcissism for an interest in the community.

Bertrand Russell (1872-1970)

British Philosopher

It is a tremendous irony that our system of government is arguably the best ever conceived by any people in history, and yet, at the same time, in the eyes of most Americans, it is so flawed. We elect politicians to run our government, the most important responsibility in our society and one, which should command the greatest respect, but we hold them up, as a group, to much scorn and derision. A few are greatly admired and respected, but, as a class, politicians are held in low esteem by the American people. Why?

If politicians are held in such contempt, not so is our Constitution. This instrument is viewed with great reverence in our society. Is it perfect? No, not really. Are there changes that the people might like to make? Probably. What kind of changes? And what about political parties? Are they good or bad or even necessary? To whom are they accountable? Do they really serve America well?

What about the bureaucracy that runs the nuts and bolts of our system? And the lobby that seems to lead so many of our officeholders in the direction of special interests? That, of course, leads to the question of our election system, money and fairness.

Are we really served well by the system as it works today? There are many weighty questions facing us concerning the way we govern ourselves, and they all start with the document on which we base our political life.

"We, the people of the United States…" begins the document on which we base our entire system of government and, for all practical purposes, our society. Since today's government has so much influence on every other facet of our lives, it is a consideration in almost everything we do. So, it is only right that the document defining such an all-encompassing system of self-rule should emanate from the people. But does it come from the people, and how much "self" is in the self-rule.

The Constitution of the United States of America is probably one of the greatest documents ever written for the purpose of defining a system of self-government. It has been hailed as the inspiration for countless other similar founding documents around the world, and there can be no doubt of the positive impact it has had on the human condition, politically and socially speaking, around the globe, but most especially here in the homeland of its authors.

When the diverse backgrounds, interests and philosophies of the authors are considered, it is almost unbelievable that this charter was composed at all, let alone in the short time and critical atmosphere of the new American States of the 1780's. At the Constitutional Convention the differences were great and the opposing positions were strong on a number of issues, not the least of which was the sovereignty of the States, especially the small ones.

The resulting debates drew fiery speeches and sometimes enflamed passions and distrust. Some wanted a King, most did not. Some wanted continued confederation, many did not. It is safe to assume that few envisioned the united country we are today.

In the end, though, many compromises were made, such as the two Houses of the Congress, one with representation based on population, the other with equal representation for each State.

Nevertheless, even with the compromises meant to assuage even the most ardent of the holdouts, a selling job was necessary over a period of several years to persuade enough of the State legislatures to adopt the Constitution.

Note that it was the State legislatures that ratified it, not the people. The people of the United States have never ratified the Constitution or any amendments by an actual vote, although millions have ratified it with blood over the more than two centuries of expansion and wars of various periods.

There is no doubt that Americans cherish and support the Constitution, or that we depend on it to defend our individual interests in American society as a whole. It and the courts that interpret and continually define it are our only defense against government itself, even one that we elect.

But the Constitution might never have been adopted in the first place, had a popular vote been necessary. Strong opponents might have waged a better campaign against it in a popular poll. State legislatures had a difficult time in some States, with sometimes belligerent outbursts from members who distrusted the idea of a strong central government with authority above their own.

Some votes to ratify passed with only slim majorities, and some only with the knowledge that the Bill of Rights was coming to soothe their concerns over having basic civil liberties included.

Still, many people who were not in the legislatures had concerns as well. The instrument has its faults to many. Loose definitions and construction allow changing interpretations by the courts to accommodate changing social conditions and just the passage of time, but they also fail to describe adequately to some exactly what the rights and obligations in the Constitution are.

What are freedom of speech, religion and press? Are they total or limited in any way? The Constitution does not say. How about the right to bear arms? What about illegal search and seizure? And what is cruel and unusual punishment?

The ambiguities in the Constitution exacerbated the conditions leading up to the Civil War, and they fuel the controversies we see today in the issues of abortion, civil rights, capital punishment and a host of others.

There are legal scholars in America today who would seek an opportunity to have a Constitutional Convention to fine tune our national charter to rid it of inadequacies such as these, but others worry that such tampering might also bring moves at the convention to change or delete some basic rights that most Americans have come to hold dear.

And, if the people had to ratify the new version, there would be a vicious campaign from all sides contesting every word. The public debate would be a black hole in society, sucking everything else into the abyss.

There is no doubt the people would want changes. Talk has been around for decades on a number of provisions in the Constitution that would not pass muster today, or at least not in present form.

Most Americans today would demand a balanced budget amendment, since our elected officials have proven for decades that they have no concept of budget management. From the first time a crisis required deficit spending, every political issue important to this politician or that, especially if it might affect re-election, became a crisis of such demand.

We on the bottom are tired of paying for such political inadequacies and mismanagement. It is time to ask our elected "leaders" to lead responsibly or pay a price for failure. The people would certainly require responsibility in the Constitution for spending and taxation to be defined in such a way as to obligate those who pass on such issues to be held accountable for the outcome of their actions.

The people would want many changes in the basic law of our land to reflect their dissatisfaction with the way national government is currently operated. But that is not all.

Contemporary Americans have other concerns as well, and they are not all about government operations. Many in America think the courts have gone too far in their attempts to strengthen the "wall of separation" between church and state.

The originators of the Constitution seemed to want to prevent government from imposing any religion above any other, but todays courts have built this intent into one to prevent anybody from exercising any religious beliefs at any public forum. Most people in the U.S. see no harm in such minor religious exercises as praying at a public meeting, or blessings by clergy, or holiday displays on public property during Christmas, Hanukkah or Ramadan.

We, the people, might change the religious freedom in our Constitution to one protecting us more from government interference in the free exercise of religion. We, the people, might also want a change in the freedom of speech provision to provide freedom from speech that hurts, such as that of vicious hate groups who promote little "for" anyone and much "against" others.

There is no value to any society in allowing anyone to say vicious things about or against someone else, if the remarks have no point to be made on any issue and are obviously intended merely to cause pain or anguish. No person's freedom of speech should be permitted to take away another's right to peaceful existence. Such a rewriting of free speech, of course, would demand a careful scrutiny to avoid the other extreme of denying free exchange of real ideas.

The press does more for this exchange, that of ideas, than possibly any other vehicle in our society. We on the bottom would be especially uninformed were it not for the free press. Nevertheless, there are those who might certainly be expected to call for more responsible regulation of the media, especially the social media.

The advent of almost universal access to the internet has allowed every participant to exercise a degree of input into this equally universal press. Information now travels almost instantaneously around the world. Atrocities that used to go unnoticed for months or even years now spur instant outrage around the globe.

Freedom of the press, as it has been interpreted in the United States, unfortunately had allowed the press to become what it was always called….the fourth estate, that is, a fourth branch of our government. Its influence in our government continues to be undeniable, and yet, since it is unelected, it is unaccountable for its failures and errors. However, the internet seems to have blunted the effects of the 'legitimate' press somewhat because of the sheer volume of information accessible to almost everyone.

Although leaders in the field would assert they are accountable to their public through sales and advertising revenues, they would also say in most markets today the lack of choice among newspapers is almost totally balanced by internet news choices. And choosing among radio and television stations is really a choice between personalities or appearance.

The only potential bright spot would be the talk shows, if they weren't dominated by radical left or radical right and glitzy entertainers more interested in ratings and money than real information for the public.

For so long newspapers were the biggest disappointment. They had the daily contact with most who wanted to be informed, and they used their "in" to spread editorial views that supported or attacked our system in ways that so rarely reflected the true concerns of real people who had to live with the results.

One of the greatest abuses was the editorial endorsement of candidates and issues. Editors like to say they have a better, more insightful perspective of candidates, since they have the opportunity to see them and hear them more than the average person, and sometimes they can have a private conversation with the candidates, too. Never mind that their editorial will most assuredly reflect their own values and concerns, which may not closely resemble those of their average readers.

Opposing opinions of comparable weight were not given equal exposure, and since most communities are served by only one major newspaper, the public went wanting. The same held true on issues. The editorial would reflect the views of an editor or staff which traveled in circles most readers don't know. Editorial writers are seldom everyday types who relate to the average American.

In fact, in attitude, they seem to resemble more the politician or bureaucrat. They know more than we do; they see more than we do; they are smarter than we are; and they want to enlighten us. What is wrong with just reporting the news of the day and allowing ordinary people to draw their own conclusions?

Yes, we, the people on the bottom, would probably change the freedom of the press provisions, too. If the press is going to campaign on candidates and issues, it should have the same restrictions and requirements as other institutions, who do the same. And with the World Wide Web has imposed those limits by its very existence. Now we are all news reporters. We are all editorial writers with access to thousands or millions.

The press can now be held to the same high standards of conduct it seems to demand from every other sector of our society. And we now have our own means to counter the influence of the legitimate press. Still, we would want to maintain that access and balance in a 'revised' Constitution. We on the bottom who depend on both types of press expect no less.

No doubt some would want other changes in the Bill of Rights. A great many would prefer a closer definition of the right to bear arms, though the National Rifle Association likes the looseness of the present provision. The wave of hand guns and automatic weapons and violence in our society would indicate some remedial action is necessary.

And the fact that some criminals "get off" on technicalities seems to call for a review of the illegal search and seizure clauses, although the modern threat of international terrorism gives us all cause for concern. We on the bottom would like to have a better definition of cruel and unusual punishment, since we have to pay for whatever punishment is carried out. Expecting elected officials to remedy these deficiencies has proven unrealistic.

Congress itself is wanting. Not all of the problems in our system stem from the Bill of Rights. The structure of our government is too unwieldy and, in many respects, really unaccountable to the people it serves, and who pay the bill.

The idea of the bicameral legislature has served us well. The fact that every State but Nebraska has a similar legislative makeup is testimony to the efficacy of the concept. Still, all the others are population based, under the "one man, one vote" rule. Why should the United States Senate continue to provide more representation to small States than to the large ones?

When the Constitution was written, the concern of then small, sovereign States that they might suffer tyranny at the hands of larger States led them to oppose the document until a compromise gave them equality in at least one House of the Congress. At the time this was probably reasonable, but today it is not.

First, the legislature no longer picks Senators from any State. They are all elected by popular vote. Since they are elected by the people, they should represent people, not States. Second, there are now fifty States, with diverse, and yet, quite common interests. Communications and travel ease in the twentieth century make all the States more alike than different.

Besides, we are not a collection of States; we are since the Civil War a nation, a people. It is possible today for a minority of the States to make a majority in the Senate. That does not serve the nation well. It also encourages the continued call by some for "States' Rights". That issue was settled in 1865. It is time for a change.

This might be the right place to discuss the District of Columbia. Not only is it a great argument against equal State representation in the Senate, since, if it became a State, it would have two Senators to influence to course of the nation, but it brings us to the issue of Statehood itself.

When the District of Columbia was formed, Virginia and Maryland gave up land from their own territory, (Virginia's portion was later returned to the state) and it was agreed that the territory would be apart from all States so that the federal government would not be in any State, thus eliminating any jealousy arising from domicile of the seat of government. All agreed.

Now, of course, political situations changing as they will, there are those in the District and those without who say the people of D.C. deserve to have a full vote in the government, and that means statehood. Nonsense!

If they want to vote for representation, they should vote for that in the State they would reside in, if the District had not been formed. For most, that would mean voting for a Maryland congressman and two Maryland Senators. Or, better still, give the territory back officially.

The government of the District of Columbia is left to the Congress at present, which delegates it to a local government under provisions passed by Congress. It is also paid for by considerable federal tax dollars. The best solution is to dissolve the District of Columbia and let Washington be a city in Maryland.

Most of us on the bottom would find that more palatable. This will continue be an issue in coming national elections. It will be interesting to read the planks in the platforms of the two major parties.

Our Constitution did not even mention political parties, and, yet, they have an overwhelming influence on the direction of our government, and, indeed, of our society itself. The first major parties arose out of the divisions at the Constitutional Convention.

Those that wanted a strong federal government formed the Federalist Party; those who preferred stronger emphasis on individual rights and less government involvement in local and

State affairs opted to join the new Democratic Republicans. The growth of our federal system ultimately made the theme of the Federalist Party moot, and it died.

The Whig Party replaced it as a major political force in young America, but it never had a true partisan philosophy. Meanwhile, under Andrew Jackson, the Democratic Republicans became just Democrats and adopted a party philosophy similar in many respects to today's Democratic Party, notwithstanding the obvious differences in time period issues.

The Whig Party's lack of the glue that holds parties together did not keep it from being a major contender for several decades in American political life, but it finally gave way to the new Republican Party in the 1850's. The Republican Party had a philosophy founded mostly in one hot issue…..slavery, or more precisely the abolition of slavery.

The party was so strong for the fifty years following the Civil War that some thought the Democratic Party would not survive. In fact, from 1860 to 1932 only Grover Cleveland and Woodrow Wilson managed to crack the seeming invincibility of the Republicans. And Wilson won primarily because a disgruntled Teddy Roosevelt and his Progressive Party drained enough votes from Taft to give Wilson the victory with a plurality of votes.

Franklin Roosevelt finally put some teeth back into the Democratic Party with a philosophy of serving the average American worker. He actually adopted much of the philosophy of his uncle Teddy. This has persisted until today, although the Party's coalition of various special interest groups has put workers, or more specifically, organized labor, in a minority in party influence.

The Republican Party, meanwhile, has attracted a reputation of a "conservative" party as opposed to the "liberals" in the Democratic Party. It would seem, therefore, that there is obvious choice for voters in the United States in almost any election at any level. Not necessarily so.

The facts show that today's American voter is more turned off on political parties than at any time in our history. When the contribution the two party system has made to this country is considered, it is hard to imagine what might have happened to turn the people on the bottom away from party membership. To gain understanding we must realize what attracted people to parties in the first place.

Historically, parties have always seemed to represent strong stands on government style and big issues that had to do with governing. Modern American politics is different. Both parties have adopted stands on divisive social issues such as abortion, gay rights, racial discrimination and a host of others. These have more to do with social attitudes than with governing.

At the same time, leadership in both parties together with the elected officials from both have proven that they are incapable of responsible governing, that is, making decisions to run the government so that it serves the interests of the people who are paying the tab. In other words, there seems to be little difference between the parties on issues of governing style.

Liberal and conservative have little meaning to a people who observe that neither seems able to make government work. With the differences between them seeming more gray than black or white, the parties offer little today philosophically to anyone except the radical elements on the social issues.

So the so called religious right finds the Republican Party comfortable as do the big business interests and the anti-Feminists, anti-Gays, anti-Civil Rights people and so on. On the other side the Feminists, Pro-Choicers, Gay Rights Activists and the other left wing groups seem to dominate the Democratic Party.

With the Republicans leaning hard right and the Democrats leaning hard left, their nominees for various offices draw increasing disenchantment from average voters who are more centrist.

The basic reason for parties, therefore, seems almost lost. To the people on the bottom the most important function of a party is to present ideas in the forum so that the best may be selected, and the country as a whole benefits. To the party leader, the most important function of the party is to make sure its candidates are elected.

That means making concessions sometimes to fringe groups who do not make a part of the majority of the party, but whose votes could make a difference in electing the candidates. This then accents the goals of the minority fringe group and gives them equal status with those of the majority in the party.

Those toward the center in the party then feel uncomfortable and leave the party, and in the process leaving the party leaning more toward the extreme that caused the shrinkage, thus causing further discomfort and more diminishment, and the cycle continues.

And now, most voters in this nation feel alienated from the parties and are not members. In addition, because of the cycle both parties are even more beholden to their fringe groups.

What can be done to reverse this trend and remedy the situation? Do we want to fix it? Do we still need political parties? What need do they fill? The answer goes back to their origins. Of course, they are useful. They offer some valuable services.

The first thing parties bring to the system is stability. Some countries of the world where there are multiple parties strong enough to command some allegiance have serious problems in government stability. Italy is still the best example of a strong western style government weakened by too many strong parties, but none strong enough to govern. Fifty governments in fifty years bear this out.

Two strong parties have proven to be the best stabilizer for representative democratic government. The United States has been from the beginning a strong two party system. Whenever a new strong party emerged here, one of the old ones died soon after, leaving once again two strong parties.

Political parties also offer the best talent screening and development system available for the cost. Notwithstanding the problem of favoring loyalty sometimes over ability, the parties have the best mechanisms for finding talent and ability and moving it to the front.

They present to the public able persons for consideration and approval. The opportunity afforded these individuals shows first at entry level usually, then increasingly higher levels, the capabilities they have to govern. This training program would be difficult without parties.

If every person interested in public service had to enter without a party, a benefactor would have to be found. The public would have to be informed as to the philosophy of the candidate through expensive advertising. Lacking resources the average person of ability might never be able to serve in public office.

Only the rich or their protégés could attain office and we as a nation would be poorly served indeed. There would have been no Jackson, Lincoln or Truman. We would have been denied some of the best leadership in the world at different times due only to means. What a loss!

Parties, therefore, are an important part of our system, if it is to work at its best. But we must make some changes if they are to serve at their optimum level. Too often party leaders make decisions which may or may not represent the feelings of the majority of their members. These decisions, especially those affecting campaign rules and election conduct, need to be governed by laws that make the leadership truly accountable for their decisions.

Civil law must insure that party leaders abide by their own parties' governing charters and rules. There must be penalties enforceable through the law for serious infractions. In this way the charter of a party may be treated under the law as a contract among the members, and the leaders will be accountable to the members much as corporate officers and board members are to stockholders.

And, just as there are ways to remove errant officers from a company, there should be a mechanism for removing high ranking party officials when a majority of the members wish to do so. This might also be said of high elected office holders as well.

Just one comment on recent court decisions about money in politics: When money dominates the whole system, the people will lose control of the outcome. Too many people are so easily swayed by nefarious comments in the media. That can tilt the balance anyway the money interests direct. The people lose.

If enough voters want to remove a congressman or Senator, there should be a workable recall provision available, and even the President and Vice-President should not be above such a control by the public. After all, it is our government, and if we choose to make a change in mid-term for some obviously important reason (It would have to be very urgent to prompt the efforts necessary to mount such a move), such a procedure should be provided by our law.

The procedure for such a party control should be provided at the earliest, if we are to save the two-party system as we know it. Members who feel they control their own party will stay in it and work to make it better. The accountability must be absolute and, though not so easy as to make it trite and commonplace, as that could further weaken parties, still easy enough that committed members would be able to force necessary changes.

At the same time State and National parties should not be so strong that they prohibit local community based parties which address only local issues. Most local political activity involves mere branches of national parties.

Since the national parties have very few platform stands on issues that are meaningful to local communities and their leaders, the identification with the national parties does little to clarify the local debate. People are urged to vote for candidates because of their party's views on foreign affairs or the domestic economy, when the real issues are about community planning and development, or services or safety, or parks and recreation, or any number of other issues having no relationship to lofty national or state concerns.

It should be easier for local political activists to form local parties to address local concerns, and to have their parties recognized by election authorities. Members should be allowed to belong to a local party and to a national party without any real affiliation between the two parties.

Presently national party rules allow membership only to those who do not belong to any other party. This narrows the path for entry into the political arena and narrows control to the leadership of the national parties. As such, it is an invitation to cronyism.

"Paying dues" is the name for it. Cronyism is a more appropriate term. This and nepotism have given us some of the most incompetent public servants available. Only a few are needed for the bad apple effect.

Public and party officials cannot be blamed for wanting to maximize their control. So, when an opening appears for a new appointment, they naturally want to put a loyalist into the position. That may be a relative or a close, loyal colleague. In either case, the new appointee will be more loyal to the politician who helped in the appointment than to the public.

The result is less efficiency and more politics in government. In the case of elected positions which become vacant, the best approach is always where possible to have an election. The people cannot be wrong. The matter of appointed bureaucrats is very different.

There can be no question that our government is bloated beyond what is necessary to provide the services needed by the American people. Most of the operations were fully justified when they were created, and few would argue the good that many have done over the years of their need.

But "their need" in many cases has long since dissipated. And yet, they continue to be funded. Why? In most cases, they are allowed to continue, especially on the federal level, because some member of Congress chairs a committee or subcommittee that deals with that particular office or position, and to eliminate the office would eliminate the need for the committee and, with it, of course, the need for the position of the Congressman who chairs it.

No member of the Congress wants to take a position from another member, because the situation may someday be reversed. In this case the golden political rule is, "Do not do unto other members that which you do not wish them to do unto you", especially within the same party.

And so, bureaus, departments and offices continue to be funded long after the need for their services has disappeared, and the Congress and one administration after another promise to reduce government mismanagement and spending. When the numbers are in the billions and trillions, they lose meaning.

Even on the local level, millions are treated like Monopoly money, so it is no surprise that our national leaders treat our money as if it were not real. It does not come out of their pockets. Perhaps, if all elected officeholders at all levels were required to be paid only out of surplus funds, there would always be an adequate surplus. Surely, there would be no federal deficit and no federal debt.

And if members of Congress were paid according to national average individual income, there would be a great effort in Washington to insure an ever increasing average individual income level throughout the United States. One thing is for sure; unnecessary government offices would be eliminated, and efficiency would become the only measure in deciding which would stay and which would go.

Those of us on the bottom might offer some suggestions. But realistically, we would probably start with the Internal Revenue Service, even though we all know it is necessary.

The IRS has been viewed by many Americans almost as a modern day Gestapo, due to its lack of observance of basic due process provisions. Although Congress has in recent years addressed some of the problems, there is still much to do to win the respect of the

American people, if not their affection, for this sometimes ruthless tax collector. There seems always to be a candidate of some office calling for the elimination of the IRS.

We have a voluntary tax collecting system in this country, and that is a preferable way, when one considers what is used in many other countries of the world, and we certainly need some entity to enforce the law. But that does not mean we should violate our own civil protections under the Constitution in order to do so.

Most Americans have heard the horror stories of IRS seizure of business property, putting the business owner and employees out of work, when other means might have prompted collection of delinquent taxes and retained the jobs and economic benefits of the business in the affected community.

And we have heard of people losing their homes and all their possessions, only to find that there was an error, and it is too late to rectify it. Proper controls and required use of due process would protect the rights of the taxpayer, while insuring government collection of legitimate taxes.

The IRS, the FBI, the CIA, the whole alphabet of U.S. government bureaus and offices needs the controlling hand of those elected by the people to protect them from the abuses that have been so widespread in recent times. Many times elected leaders have complained that the bureaucrats are out of control and that they really run the government.

Elected leaders may come and go, but the bureaucrats are always there. They advise and inform the elected; they work for the elected, but they are the ones who really know what is going on in their respective agencies. The elected leadership relies on the judgment and experience of the bureaucrats to such a great degree, that we on the bottom can only assume that our leaders are allowing the bureaucrats to make the actual decisions on policy that the leaders carry out.

That is not what we elected them to do. They are supposed to exercise their own judgment of what we want or need to be done.

182

If they are not capable, they should step aside and allow someone in who can do the job.

Of course, that is unrealistic, and we all know that. As the opening quote of this chapter says, most in office long ago lost their commitment to serving those who sent them to office.

That is not to say they never had such a commitment. Almost all did. The voters knew it when they elected them the first time. Unfortunately, they began to read too much of their own campaign literature, and believed everything they read. They forgot that such promotional material is not supposed to be a complete analysis of a person, just a positive summary, without the warts.

Nevertheless, the self-worship sets in, and the self-indulgence soon follows. Before long, staff is doing the job, and the elected is spending more time with those who can reinforce a bloated self-concept, the money people who feed their campaigns. This is probably the best argument for term limits, although there are many who realize that term limitation is not the solution.

Although it certainly rids us of useless politicians who have grown fat and lazy at the public trough, it unfortunately costs us some highly skilled, hard working veterans at the same time. The need is not for term limits; it is for informed voters and limited campaign hype.

However, if we are to have term limits, let the limit be one term. It is obvious, our founders thought of public service as an interruption of one's career. They thought patriots should be willing to give up several years to serve the country or community and return afterward to their career or enterprise.

With the population we have, we will never run out of reasonably capable candidates to replace those serving. It could be easily argued that we could move across America, randomly selecting representatives and Senators from the streets of our communities, and we would not fare worse than what we have now.

That said, the biggest barrier between an informed electorate and public-serving public servants is the organized lobby. Lobbyists work for special interests, not for the public good. They are paid to present a slanted view of their issues in order to direct the outcome in favor of their clients.

The intolerable part of the equation is the attention given these vultures by the people we expect to serve our interests, just because we elected them. They obviously put more stock in those who financed them than in the ones with the votes.

The Roman orgy mentality in the lobby of almost every legislature including Congress is a disgrace to the American people and our way of government. That we as a people tolerate it is an abomination second only to those we only half seriously these days refer to as our elected government.

Even those among our legislators who recognize this unethical and immoral influence in our governing affairs for what it is do not have the courage to stand and fight until it is changed, since they would have to fight all the monied interests in their next election and take a chance on losing.

The job has become so important that doing the job has lost its meaning. Those of us on the bottom pay the cost of government, and we don't have enough left to pay for the cost of campaigns. The lobbyists, however, have an almost infinite amount available for those who "cooperate" in their causes. Those funds can defeat even the noblest candidate.

The advertising media can sway voters into thinking whatever is needed about a specific candidate to elect their choice. The American people have grown cynical and lazy, when it comes to studying the issues and candidate qualifications. The easy road is to absorb the advertising hype, the glitz, and vote for the familiar name.

The Citizens United case was a Supreme Court gift to the big money interests across the nation. They now can spend almost unlimited funds with no disclosure to the public of contributors or operatives. They can manipulate the public into voting for their candidates, who do the most for them.

Ninety-eight percent of the time, that is the incumbent, and the incumbents are the problem. Yes, some of them are able and capable. They are even dedicated. But, mixed in among them, are so many who have been absorbed into the system and are comfortable. They look forward to long careers and the best retirement benefits in the United States.

No private business pension can compare. No wonder they fear losing an election. If everyone in America could look forward to a similar pension program, no one would ever want to go to heaven.

Much needed legislation is buried or mutilated beyond recognition because these self-dedicated non-public servants sell their political souls to the lobbyists for campaign money. The only special interest that is ignored is that strange animal known as the majority, the average people, those on the bottom.

They have only their vote to offer. And so another extra branch of government —-the lobby—- has a greater say than the self-governing people we like to think we are.

Only a right of national referendum can solve this problem. Those we elect will not stop the flood of money from the special interests. They will not return their accountability to the voters. We are the only ones who might be able to, but only if we can take the initiative —- the initiative referendum.

We must have the power as a people to initiate legislation from the people up when necessary. Only then can we, the people, be sure that something so necessary as ethical reform actually takes place. We need this right.

With it we could reform the election campaign process, require balanced budgets and so much more to make our own government responsive and responsible to us. Ultimately, perhaps our elected officials might be reminded that, in America, we are the government.

But, how can our elections be reformed? It has been discussed and debated for decades. The principal concern is, of course, the flow of such enormous amounts of money and the corruption of the process by that money. No one could argue that the biggest improvement in the process would involve the control of this one problem. But, there are other improvements that could be made.

It would help if it were easier to register and vote. Cumbersome registration regulations in the various States should be replaced with the easiest possible registration system. Almost every adult drives, and it seems logical that, since we have to register drivers, it would be easier to make such registration do double duty as voter registration as well.

The State of Washington recently installed such a system. It seems rational, and it will be interesting to see how it works out for them. Of course, that is an opposite approach from states that continually restrict or inhibit voting rights, in an obvious attempt to limit minorities and sway elections.

Or we might even use birth records and naturalization to register. No matter what system we adopt, it should be one that provides the greatest ease for voters to register. Maximum participation generally yields better government. It also works against incumbents. That is why most do not favor such easy rules.

But, of late, it seems there is a push, especially in Republican controlled legislatures, to limit or impede registration and voting procedures, in order to reduce voting by certain demographic groups. African Americans, Hispanic Americans and the elderly are targeted, as they more often tend to vote for Democrats.

In addition, the Supreme Court not long ago gutted an important section of the Voting Rights Act. That change now allows more manipulation of the voting process by states that have a history of limiting voting rights of minorities. We need to take the necessary steps to open the voting process to everyone.

By the same token, we should make it easier for potential candidates to run for office. In most States it is easier for a party candidate to run than for an independent. There is no reason for this, other than to protect party candidates from possibly tougher competition.

It certainly is not to protect the American people from additional choices. The more choices available in any election, the better will be the outcome for the voters. The biggest problem we have most of the time is a scarcity of contenders and really no choice. Often there is only one candidate on the ballot for a particular position in small communities.

What a tragedy that others who may be interested in public service are deterred by such a discouraging system. It should take no more than twenty-five signatures on a petition for a local office, whether for partisan or independent candidacy.

And what of voting itself? Why do we still vote on a working day in mid-week in twentieth century America? It would seem to make more sense, if we held our elections on weekends and allowed voters to vote on Saturday and Sunday. The votes could be tallied on Monday.

This is being done in more and more communities and states. Public pressure has forced expansion of absentee or early voting. And early voting has expanded into weekends, thus making participation more available to those with challenging work schedules.

The ease of voting encourages more to take part, and, once again, more participants might yield better results. And, where possible, a majority should be required to win an election. If multiple candidates divide votes so that no one has a majority, there should be a run-off election held within weeks to allow voters to choose from the top two candidates in the regular election.

This would give us public servants who would have enough support to bolster their positions (hopefully our positions) on issues. At least it is closer to a mandate than a plurality would be.

This would surely help a President. Not many have won without a majority of voters, but it has happened, and it has to be a handicap for any President when dealing with a Congress full of members, most of whom had clear majorities in their own elections. Such a run-off election would serve to give the new President the mandate status necessary to be seen as an equal by Congress.

This would seem a good point to discuss Presidential primary elections. The present system gives too much weight to small States that are not necessarily representative of the nation as a whole.

Too often, however, the primaries in the early States eliminate good candidates who might have fared much better had they had their initial campaign decided in larger States where more issues are considered.

The proposal for a regional primary system seems the most reasonable. This would allow candidates to campaign in a limited geographical area, and give those with limited resources a better chance to take their issues to the voters.

The whole country would be better served, if we all had more opportunities to choose. Many attractive candidates are eliminated by our current system long before California, Ohio and Illinois have a say. They run out of money before they run out of time.

Money is the prime ingredient in any campaign, thus, the influence of the lobbyists and special interest action funds. If we are to stop the wholesale buying of elections by special interest groups, we must limit the money they can provide for or against candidates. In order to do that, we have to create a better system for election conduct.

The easiest and least expensive way to accomplish this, in spite of what incumbents would have us believe, is to have government sponsored campaigns. Every time this option comes up, it is confronted by the same arguments from the members of Congress and the various State legislatures. They say the people will never support it.

Of course, the people won't support it, when these legislators discuss paying for it out of current tax revenues. But there is a plausible and acceptable way to fund it, at least in the eyes of the voters.

First, require all media to provide certain information coverages on candidates and issues as a cost of doing business in a democratic America. They claim their first obligation is to inform; let them live up to that claim. Next we must limit the amounts that are spent on campaign expenses of all types.

In order to balance between incumbents and challengers, some value must be given to incumbency. Everyone knows it is an advantage, and there must be a way to measure reasonably the empirical value of incumbency. Then, in order to be fair to a challenger, that difference must be given as an added allowance in expense to a challenger.

Perhaps the government printing offices could take time out from printing all the useless records they make every day as a paper memorial in most cases to current officeholders, in order to print information packets on all candidates for the voters. These could be mailed prior to election, so that everyone could become familiar with all the candidates from a cold, factual, non-hype piece of literature.

These are not all the answers to the problems we face in our election system. They may not provide any reasonable alternative, but they along with other ideas should be explored. Something should be done. No more of the wringing of the hands and the shaking of the heads and the defeated looks of hopeless resignation to no change at all.

We on the bottom deserve better. We deserve the opportunity to find the best available, not the best incumbent available. That is no choice, as we have all seen, over and over.

One more note about the intolerable lobbyist influence on government and elections. Many special interest groups receive tax breaks that are not available to voters (taxpayers) on the bottom.

Why should they and their supporters receive preferential tax treatment?

Some violate the spirit of fairness in taxation even further. One good example —- The Women's Political Caucus movement. Their goal they say is to help elect women to public office; not candidates who favor women's issues, just women candidates. That is gender discrimination. No group supporting the idea of electing only male candidates would be treated by the system so kindly.

Funding for publicly supported campaigns could be found in taxing such groups and for that matter all campaign funds. Why not grant a tax break to those who donate small sums to candidates. Then, tax the campaign funds themselves in order to fund public information campaigns to inform voters on their candidates.

In view of some of the obscene amounts left over in campaign funds, maybe those funds should be required to donate all monies left over above certain reasonable carryover levels to the national campaign fund. Some of these funds have hundreds of thousands, even millions, of dollars on hand for some future election, or as a fund for various uses for the officeholder or candidate.

As stated earlier, we could provide un-flowered, unscented raw information on each candidate, so the voters could examine only relevant facts pertaining to the individuals and the issues. An informed public is the greatest threat to poor candidates and a poorly operating system.

We on the bottom have been abused by this system, and the three branches of government have been equally reluctant to move for change. Even the courts do little, given their limited opportunities to examine our electoral mess. They have quite often exacerbated the problems.

The courts could use a little self-scrutiny. We, the people, are not fully satisfied with their performance either. Most of the trouble with the judicial system was discussed earlier, but the federal courts, especially the Supreme Court, present additional frustration for the American people.

The first objection has to be life tenure. Such an open term leaves too much chance for mental degeneration of a given justice to influence decisions affecting all Americans. This is ridiculous. There is no reason not to require retirement at some advanced age. Many State courts require retirement at age seventy or seventy-five.

Furthermore, if federal judges stray far from the acceptable performance desired by the American people, there is no system for removal other than the impeachment process, and it is rare for Congress to take such action, especially in a case that may be political in nature.

Still, the American people should have some mechanism for removing a federal judge or Supreme Court Justice who seems to violate their sense of justice. Had such a means been available, no doubt several would have been removed following the Dred Scott decision.

Perhaps the Civil War might have been averted, or fought earlier with fewer casualties and less national trauma. Who knows what would happen now with abortion, civil rights and other hotly debated issues at the fore?

Those who say this would politicize the courts too much, forget that they are already politicized by the politicians who appoint and confirm them. One needs only to have watched Senate confirmation hearings in recent years, especially those of Robert Bork and Clarence Thomas, to realize the people of the United States could hardly do a worse job of politicizing the courts.

And, besides, if the courts are going to be politicized, should they not then reflect the political bent of people over that of the politicians?

The politicians seem more distant than ever from the people they serve. That is especially true of our representatives in Congress and, to a lesser degree, those in State legislatures.

No wonder! A visit to Washington, D.C. has to impress any visitor, with all the construction and improvements that are taking place in our nation's capital. The same is true in Harrisburg, Sacramento, Lansing or any of the State capitals. It would seem that the economy is booming everywhere.

Our legislators must, indeed, have the impression most of the time that everything is rosy back home as well. It is sad that they have forgotten that everyone else doesn't live and work in this environment of affluence and progress. The distance has certainly grown between the representative and the represented.

The people on the bottom in the United States have grown cynical and distrustful of their own government and those they have entrusted with its operation for the common good. The government designed to serve us has become a giant beast that has instead made us its servants.

We work to provide it the money to create more and more of itself as more of a burden to us. We choose people we trust to change it, to tame it to serve us, and they become part of the beast. It is as if it were some alien life form, absorbing all who come into contact with it.

It is viewed by many with resignation to its awesome power and seeming invincibility. The Constitution was designed to provide the first government on earth to originate from and truly serve the people it governed. Some day it may again become that.

There are a growing number of people who think the solution is to reduce the size of government. There certainly are adjustments of size that could be made just by reducing the 'fat' of government. But, wholesale cutting of services is not the same as trimming the fat. That actually reduces the real services the government ought to provide. The so-called Tea Party is not the solution.

There are arising from among us new, bold and better candidates who are slowly taking the offices from those, who do not deserve to hold them. When enough good people are elected, and if they too are not corrupted, then the government of the people, by the people and, most especially, for the people will bring a better day. We on the bottom await that day.

GHOSTS

The Haunting of America

"I am the Ghost of Christmas Past." "Long past?" inquired Scrooge... "No. Your past."

Charles Dickens 1812-1870

A Christmas Carol

How many times has each of us acted out of the fear of repeating a past mistake? We all, it seems, fear our past. It is as if it had a life of its own and could come back at anytime to exact a price for our memories. We all have these ghosts that haunt our every action. We do things or don't do things according to our fear or encouragement from past experiences.

It is no wonder that our national psyche can suffer from the same anxiety. Is this factor a positive or negative one? What makes a common national past? How can we cope with the good and bad memories we share as a people? How are these ghosts affecting us now, and how can we be sure of their effect on our future?

Sigmund Freud would have loved to put America on his couch and listen to the chatter of a neurotic national soul. We as a people are plagued by the deeds of generations gone by; not just by the results of those actions or inactions, but by the spirits of the times. We cannot forget. We seem compelled to act always in a way predetermined by our national history more than our promising future.

America, like Dickens' Scrooge, must somehow strike a balance among the ghosts of our past, present and future, if we are to make a future that brings the best to all of us. The past is a lesson, or series of lessons, from which we must learn and avoid repetition of costly errors, but, on balance, the past must be less important in making decisions than the present facts, which are more relevant to current issues.

To be sure, our national memory is important and positive in helping to avoid mistakes, but it should not bring with it the fear of pursuing our dreams. Such trepidation stifles the principal spirit — - the human spirit.

It was this individual human spirit which begat the Spirit of 76. The founding of America and, with it, the American dream we share today was the high point in human achievement in the world. Amid all the darkness in human misery around the world, one light broke. That light has illuminated the world, and it was this Spirit of 76 that fueled the light. This Spirit is the most positive element in our past. It is the first, along with the Pioneer Spirit and the Spirit of opportunity, of the trinity that shaped America. Together, they are the Ghost of America Past.

For so many generations young Americans have acquired a national pride in the heroic acts of the ill-armed and unprepared colonists, who dared to challenge the most powerful empire in the world, and, through dogged determination, won a freedom unique in all the ages of history.

It was unimaginable to anyone outside the American colonies and quite a few within, that such a success could be possible. There was really no reason to expect a victorious outcome from the rebellion. Through all the hardships of Valley Forge, the many lost battles, the dead, the wounded, the discouraged deserters, the spirit remained intact, and the determination grew stronger.

These brave rebels fought on because they had nothing to which to return, except the unacceptable chains of subservience and oppression as a heritage they would pass on to their children.

But their children had a better destiny. This new world held more than new land, new fields, and new wealth. Here was new opportunity for human endeavor, a new beginning. Here was a freedom of distance from the oppressor. Here was a new attitude, one of resentment of the power that confiscated a share of the rewards without sharing in the hardship and the toil. Here was found a small taste of freedom that spawned a growing taste FOR freedom.

Here was born a people with a sense of defiance of authority not of their own making, and resistance to an overbearing force from a distant land. Here in this new world was a new breed with a new concept in human existence and a new spirit to drive them. Here had grown more than crops and cattle and discontent. Here was grown something much more valuable, something long dormant in the human soul.

Here had grown a spirit of determination, a spirit of faith in the common person's right and ability to build a future. Here was born a spirit that would inspire all peoples around the world to hope for the freedom that America found first. This spirit lives in every human being on earth, but to us Americans it is the Spirit of 76.

Our pride as Americans in the circumstances surrounding the founding of our country does not overshadow our admiration for the settlers who left the comfort of the eastern seaboard to venture west into unknown dangers to stretch the young country across the continent.

Notwithstanding the obvious injustice to the Native Americans from whom the settlers took access to land, food and an ancient free lifestyle, the hardships faced by the pioneers were real and severe. It is a tribute to the character of these early Americans that they succeeded in spite of the countless deaths from Indian attacks, disease, weather, exhaustion and the myriad of obstacles that have always faced people of vision and determination.

The view from the bottom has always been exactly that in looking up to these adventurers with enough of the Pioneer Spirit to provide the great land their children would need to build the America that is still, with all our problems today, the envy of every people in the world.

And every people in the world has sent immigrants to this land to help in building what we have today. This is a land that has always been seen as a land of opportunity. No other country in the history of this planet has been the destination for so many seeking to better their lives.

In the beginning America offered land and minerals. There was a chance to own a piece of property and, through hard work, to raise a family. This was an unheard of opportunity to most coming here, but the new concept of personal freedom was the jewel most sought. The freedom to succeed or fail based on personal efforts, not on social status or the grace of a sovereign.

Those who came saw an opportunity to build a farm, or build a business or build an industry. And these farms and businesses and industries built America. We today call this the American dream. It is the dream of building families and futures for our children.

To others who seek to join in the dream, it is called the American opportunity. This is what they seek. It is what all immigrants have sought throughout our history from the early settlers to the pioneers to the new wave that joins us even today. It is a spirit that yearns for expression and drives for achievement. It is the untiring Spirit of Opportunity.

Yes, Americans take great pride in our past. These spirits, the Ghost of America Past, are just reason for pride, and it is this pride that nurtures the hope for the future. For, if those who have faced such hardships as revolution, taming wilderness and building a nation from nothing but will can endure, surely we who dwell in relative comfort can muster the character and energy to continue to improve what they began in such hardship.

The legacy of this Ghost of America Past is the lesson of the human spirit itself, that it is unstoppable, that it is determined, that hope and vision are its children. That these offspring are alive and well in America today is testament to spirits that begat them and to those who today nourish and encourage them.

Unfortunately, they do not move among us alone. All spirits seem eternal, and there are other more sinister ghosts moving among us, haunting us with the memories of error, misjudgment and occasional failures in our past. It is not the past of our nation, but of those only who live today.

These spirits are the Ghost of America Present, and this ghost seems to be the negative side of our national psyche. After two centuries of phenomenal growth, development and achievement, we now find ourselves hesitant at every crossroad. Nary a decision is made nor an action contemplated by us as a people without the intrusion of these spirits and the discouragement they bring.

We seem to be governed more by fear of past error than by the promise of the future or even just what is right for today. We have somehow missed the lessons of our mistakes and instead fear the errors themselves.

They are over, finished, done. It is time to learn and move on. Each sin of the past must be studied and appreciated for what we can learn from it. The important ones can make us a better people, if we use them to make right judgment instead of just avoiding wrong ones by avoiding making any decisions at all.

The Ghost of Slavery is one of the malevolent spirits that haunts us even today, though it should have died one hundred fifty years ago. It might have been long buried, had everyone accepted the verdict of history and the principle of equality of human beings, but some have never accepted the notion, because either they have feelings of inferiority or superiority, or they are ignorant.

No matter the reason, the spirit survived the Civil War, Reconstruction and over one hundred years of struggle for universal civil rights. It has been the greatest obstacle to the modern Civil Rights Movement. It haunts many minority members of our society with the collective memory of the humiliating status of their ancestors, while keeping alive in many less intelligent whites the silly notion that one human being can have more worth than another.

This ghost makes quotas seem reasonable. It makes affirmative action programs necessary. It makes those in authority in many circumstances look at characteristics and features that are not relevant to the decisions they must make.

Consequently, age old wrongs are further aggravated. Tension builds between races, with black Americans distrusting whites and whites often dismissing the legitimate hopes of blacks and other minorities. This ghost is the mother of modern racism, and, unless and until she dies, she will continue to nourish her child, who grows ever stronger.

We need no further propagation of such a line. It is time we united as a people to destroy this evil spirit among us. We cannot easily move on into our future as a people until we have eliminated this unnatural, divisive spirit. More recent events have confirmed that the new century has brought this ghost with it.

As sinister as the Ghost of Slavery is, it is not alone in its negative nature. There are others. The Ghost of the Great Depression, for instance, haunts the elderly in America as no other generation could possible understand. There is a pervasive fear that hangs over every American who lived through this monstrous event in the history of the whole world.

Many were the children who begged in the streets for food to take home to destitute families. Many were the families touched by suicide of fathers who felt they were failures or mothers unable to cope with the misery of their families. Poverty and need, misery and suffering were the gifts of this spirit, along with a memory to haunt a lifetime. Today our elderly American generation lives a life stooped under the heavy mist of this spirit.

They dare not spend too much on themselves for fear of running out of money, so they miss many pleasures. They scrimp and save "just in case", and they deny themselves sometimes even necessities. Some hide money in their homes for fear of bank closings.

At the very time that modern medical science has allowed record lifespans in good health, so many cannot enjoy the additional years to the fullest because of the fear wrought of the Depression of their youth. It is an evil spirit, indeed, that robs those who have labored a lifetime of the fruits of that labor, the pleasure of enjoying life at the time of life when it can be most appreciated.

This ghost and the time that bore it are aptly named, since depression is its legacy as well. What can destroy this spirit is unimaginable, as it feeds on the memories of its victims. The ghost may only die with the generation that has lived with it.

Those of us in younger generations can offer only understanding and compassion in order to try to dull its impact on our parents and grandparents. We may not kill the spirit, but we might weaken it enough to allow its cold, dark shadow to be dispelled by the warm light of love.

But the Ghost of America has a big family, and some touch many generations. Such is the Ghost of War. Almost every generation in our history has known war. Some wars seemed just, some did not. Some had public support, some did not.

No matter what the cause, be it revolution, expansion, secession, to bring peace or to end all war, suffering was the legacy of all wars. And not all the suffering was on the battlefield.

Many who lost friends or loved ones suffered great pain. Many combatants who came home suffered great anguish over the loss of comrades, personal wounds or just the pain of the memories of their own required actions.

It is not easy for most to kill or maim, no matter how justified, and return to the innocent life of youth. Innocence, once lost, is forever lost.

Our older generation, the generation of the Great Depression, fought World War II, the most publicly supported war in our history. It was a righteous war, a just war, and they were justifiably proud to have played their part in destroying some of the evil in their world. They saved many from great suffering.

But they found some suffering for themselves. There were many killed and wounded. There were many who were scarred physically, and many who were scarred mentally and emotionally for life. They and their children have lived more than a generation under the threat of the Cold War.

The spirit of the World War and the Cold War took us into the Korean War and the Vietnam War. The spirit of righteousness left from the World War compelled us to save the world from all tyranny, including that of communism. We, therefore, had to help South Korea, and we had to help South Vietnam. At least, that is the way it was presented to the public.

But the Korean armistice left us for the first time with the feeling of a job left unfinished. There was little pride in fighting and suffering and not winning or losing, just leaving.

Korea was the first war that saw Johnny come marching home to silence instead of hurrahs. Fighting for America had lost its luster. No longer did the younger generation exhibit the zeal of their fathers for the "glory" of military service.

For generations many families had members proudly serving their country. Now a new generation was growing up questioning whether such service was so great an honor. The time was ripe for rebellion. America seems to have some kind of rebellion every hundred years. But this rebellion was not to separate ourselves from a sovereign or to secede from union. This was a generational war against authority itself.

What began as assistance to one side of a civil war in Vietnam, became a conflict of young Americans against a government run by an older generation, that the young felt would send them to fight in a far off land they did not care about, against an enemy they did not hate, for a cause they did not espouse.

Demonstrations, resistance and, sometimes, violence marked the defiance they felt. Property was destroyed; people were injured; some were even killed. The upheaval in our society was extreme.

The members of our military services were subjected to insults, degradation and sometimes injury at the hands of those who targeted them for the protests against the government they served. This nation has been emotionally crippled since that time.

No effort of the United States that involves any military activity of any kind is ever considered without casting it first under the light of Vietnam. Every instance is measured by its potential or seeming potential to turn into another Vietnam.

How pitiful in a way that the most powerful and, historically, the most militarily successful nation in the world would measure all its military actions in light of its single greatest failure! This country's moral commitment to help the helpless, save the hopeless, assist the weak and counter the strong should not be sacrificed on the altar of that single defeat. We were defeated by ourselves, not a stronger enemy.

We went to Vietnam with no real plan for victory, only defense. Politicians in Washington obstructed military efforts. Demonstrators at home undermined our resolve and the actions of our troops on the battlefield.

Justified as were their objections, the anti-war activists had a democratic system in which to change our direction. They were too impatient and too faithless to use our system to accomplish their goals. To them the end justified the means.

That is the very antithesis of our theory of democratic rule. The Baby Boomer generation was split into opposing factions on this crucial issue, and the split has remained to this day. Many on the bottom, even among those who opposed the war, feel even today that people such as Jane Fonda committed treason during that war, and they may have helped cause additional deaths and suffering among our service personnel.

Forgiveness will not come in the lifetime of this generation. She and her colleagues must seek their forgiveness from the judgment of history. The ghost of the Vietnam War is the cruelest in this family and will haunt a generation for the rest of their lives. Its legacy will affect generations to come.

And that ghost of war had children. On September 11, 2001, our homeland was attacked from within by sinister visitors from the Middle East. They commandeered planes and flew them in a Kamikazi manner into the World Trade Center in New York and the Pentagon. More than 3,000 people were killed.

The outrage spawned wars in Iraq and Afghanistan. Thousands more lives were lost, and political points were made on all sides as to whether we should have gone to such long, drawn out wars. Some thought we should have destroyed our immediate enemies and gone home.

But, a prolonged effort was made to change the way of governing in those countries to democratic systems. That brought us long conflict with enemies hiding in mountains and deserts. In addition, America itself divided into two camps, based on support or opposition to those wars.

Even today, with one of those over and the other reduced, we are still divided over them. And now we face residual war against terrorism born of age old resentment of American involvement with despotic regimes of the past in the Islamic world. That ghost of war never really leaves us.

Another ghost first recognized and acknowledged by the Baby Boomer generation is the Ghost of Poverty. This one, to paraphrase the Bible, has always been with us. It was especially strong during the Great Depression, but it never died. It has lingered for decades.

During the 1960's we declared a War on Poverty. Like so many social wars, however, this one was not serious. Only one side was really fighting, and winning——poverty. It is a strong-willed spirit. It consumes human bodies and souls.

This spirit can live in the midst of affluence, and in America it must. Even though it makes no effort to hide, the affluent often don't see it, or just don't want to see it.

Moreover, contrary to popular opinion, poverty is not cheap. It actually costs quite a lot. It costs taxpayers to maintain our massive welfare system. It costs the medical community for care for those who cannot pay. It costs law enforcement officials, insurance companies, and all of us for the additional costs of crime in America. It costs the loss of much needed human potential in terms of lost education for many gifted people who might have been doctors, engineers, scientists or any number of professionals serving human needs.

And what of the cost to our moral fabric? We cannot sacrifice such a significant portion of our human resources to apathy. They are a part of us. How can we suffer the loss of part of our being without being less for it?

If we continue to lose members of the American family to this robber, we may ultimately forfeit our place as the moral leader of the world. Much we need to help others in the world to come up to the American level, but we must begin here. Charity begins in the home.

We must care for the American family at home, before we help our neighbors in the world. It is time for a new "War on Poverty", but this time we have to fight to win. The last war promised public support, education and jobs. We gave the public support and reneged on the rest.

In the end we made welfare a generational heritage. All the poor want is a chance for the American dream. Surely, helping them achieve it, will take nothing from the rest of us. On the contrary, it may actually save us money, save our conscience and save human resources we cannot afford to lose. This ghost can be destroyed. It can be destroyed by our collective resolve. The only question is how much resolve is left in America today.

The craziest ghost haunting the Baby Boomers is the Ghost of Nostalgia. More than any group ever, the Boomers appear to be obsessed with the simple life of the 50's and 60's. Those were the days!

The birth of rock and roll, sack dresses, sneakers, ducktails, sock hops, hot cars, drive in movies and all the things that made youth innocent, happy and carefree. Maybe it is because today's youth is not innocent.

Today's children are denied the joy of carefree existence of pure childhood. They grow up too fast, having to worry about drugs, pregnancy, violence, the kind of things Boomers never worried about until the mid-sixties.

There is a certain narcotic-like pleasure in wandering through the past. The nostalgic trip through music, old TV shows and movies provides a pleasant escape from the pressures and uncertainty of today to a time when there seemed to be no cares at all.

It was not true. There were plenty of concerns, some very serious, but the perception of those "good old days" is better than the reality. Sometimes we can make the past what we want it to have been.

This ghost is the only member of the Ghost of America Present that is not all bad. The pleasant walk in this wonderful but foreign past provides the mental relief that preserves the collective sanity of a whole generation.

The bad, unfortunately, included the later part of the Boomer past, Vietnam, Watergate, protest, civil unrest, the so-called downer phase. But, by and large, the Ghost of Nostalgia is a friendly ghost. We might as well enjoy this one. It will be with us well into this century.

The final member of this family is the companion of the Ghost of Nostalgia. It is the Ghost of Assassination. Though we have had traumatic assassinations before in our life as a nation, including the murders of Abraham Lincoln, James Garfield and William McKinley, those of recent decades have seemed an assault on America itself.

The killing of John F. Kennedy in November, 1963, cut into the heart of almost every American, but it especially scarred the Baby Boomers. They were the first young Americans to take an interest in politics. JFK's charismatic personality drew them into politics like a magnet.

They felt a compulsion to join efforts on a national level to fight the social ills that plagued America. They were going to fight for civil rights, end poverty, raise educational and scientific achievement and make the second half of the twentieth century the golden age of America. The young president and his young brigade were ready for task.

Then, an assassin's bullet destroyed Camelot. That bullet struck deep at the heart of this anxious generation. Suddenly their childlike faith in America was turned to cynicism. Now, their leader dead and their faith gone, they would turn against the system that had allowed this crime against them.

Their innocence gone, they abandoned in droves the values they had once believed in. Material goods had no meaning. Success had no lure. They would seek instead to complete their drive for civil rights, an end to war, and trips through drugs to carefree existence. It would take two more decades for them to grow out of their self-made exile in their own land to take their place in today's leadership in America.

Meanwhile, the Ghost of Assassination would claim other heroes. First, Dr. Martin Luther King, Jr., the guiding light of the Civil Rights Movement was struck down, but, fortunately, the movement lived on, eventually to benefit all Americans. And it continues today, much to the credit of Dr. King, his vision and his courage.

Then Robert F. Kennedy, on the verge of being elected president, was shot down just as his brother had been. Who knows what he might have been as president?

Attempts were made on Presidents Gerald Ford and Ronald Reagan, as well as on candidate George Wallace, leaving him in a wheel chair. This ghost has haunted all Americans with the constant threat of taking our leaders and with them our security.

It is really the essence of the violence in contemporary American society. This Ghost of Assassination is a blight on modern America, but there can be no way to destroy it, since it lives within the depraved individuals who become its agents. We must be ever on guard against it, and we must hope we can intercept its efforts whenever and wherever they can be discovered.

And so are the members of the family of spirits that are the Ghost of America Present. We are haunted by the experiences of contemporary Americans as no previous nation has ever been. We make no decisions and we consider few actions of any national consequence without first considering how they relate to these traumatic spirits that drift among us.

We may, indeed, avoid repeating many mistakes, but how many opportunities will our psychotic caution cost us? How much greatness will pass us by in the darkness of our fear? Unless we can rise above our errors without sacrificing our sense of adventure and moral righteousness, we may deny future generations of Americans their chance to shine a light for the world. We must look to the Ghost of America Future if we are to remain the greatest nation on earth.

It is this ghost whose essence is the spirit of hope, that offers us respite from the negative influences of many of the spirits in the Ghost of America Present. In actuality it may be the Spirit of 76 living on today or its offspring, but either way it offers us the promise of a future built on bold adventure rather than timid avoidance.

To find this spirit we need only look to the people for her dwelling place. Principally, it is within the average American, those on the bottom, that this spirit seeks to keep the fire burning, for theirs is a dream that is pure. They seek not glory, nor even riches, but rather a better life for their children and a better land for all. Theirs is the true American Dream. It is the vision of those at the top that is distorted, probably from the combination of social altitude and distance from the masses.

Although it is those at the top who, by virtue of their leadership positions, should provide the vision for the future, they have proven time after time that they are handicapped by the narrow view of their own goals alone.

Politicians speak of vision, while their eyes are on the polls. Business leaders view the future with one eye on the bottom line. Bureaucrats see everything through the record of efficiency reports. Leaders talk about what they think the people want to hear, whether to win a vote or a sale.

But after the vote, comes the record, and after the sale comes the service. The dismal performance of most of our leaders in the United States, whether they be in public service or private business is one checkered so badly by failure as almost to obscure the few successes.

This speaks to the effectiveness of the Ghost of America Present. But those on the bottom, possessed of the spirit of hope, can and will make a difference.

At crucial times throughout our history, it has been the people who have made the difference. Sometimes the people must lead and the leaders must follow, or at least get out of the way. When leadership fails, ordinary people must step up and take the lead, exercise the necessary vision and storm the castle if necessary to provide the impetus for progress.

The American people have proven their capabilities over and over, and we have proven we have the spirit to use them to the fullest. We can fulfill the dream of the Ghost of America Past; we can overcome the Ghost of America Present; and we can surely validate ourselves through the Ghost of America Future. We, the people on the bottom, have our regrets from the past and our fears of the present, but we will move on with our hopes for the future.

America was born in chaos and forged in the fire of hardship. This land has become a monument to the will of mankind to live free or die.

Living free has won most of the battles, and many lives have been paid as the price. We have resisted the chains of tyranny and oppression, but we fight even harder to deny our own negative spirits that would haunt us into submission to the greatest tyrant of all, surrender.

Surrender to the errors of the past; surrender to the fear of the present; or, worse, surrender to despair of the future. We all recognize that our past has been not only positive, but actually miraculous in the history of this world. Our present, though fraught with difficulties, remains a beacon of light to so many trying to emerge from the darkness of oppression and deprivation.

But it is our future that promises most. With the spirit of hope and determination that is America and her people, the twenty-first century will see an America grown young again, vibrant, exuberant and filled with a certainty that her best days are still ahead.

This nation was destined by the power that created it to lead a weary world toward a better life for all humankind. Our leaders have always hoped for this, but we on the bottom have always known it. If the leaders will listen to those on the bottom, they will overcome our problems of today.

They will provide the leadership to move beyond these temporary difficulties, complex as many are, and through the spirit that conquers all that haunts us as a people, the spirit of hope, we as a nation will lead a better world, a world in which everyone has the greatest opportunity for life, liberty and the pursuit of happiness.

This may be a simplistic view, but in light of the failures of those at the top, perhaps the only view that really counts is the view from the bottom.

The spirits that I summoned up I now can't rid myself of.

Johann Wolfgang Goethe 1749-1832

The Sorcerer's Apprentice

Fear – The Driving Force in Modern America

The only thing we have to fear is – fear itself!

President Franklin D. Roosevelt

In the early 1970's a young evangelist named Pat Robertson caught the attention of many of the new generation of Americans with his style and his book, "Shout it from the Rooftop". That title referred to television antennas on the rooftops of America as a prime resource for spreading the Gospel.

Technology had been taking over in fields of entertainment and information, and now would become a primary vehicle for spreading faith. Robertson was not the first to use the media for evangelism. Preachers had been using radio and television for many years to reach more people.

But Robertson saw more. Many Christians did not participate in our political processes, as they thought politics was beneath true practice of their faith. Quite a few did not even vote. Robertson thought in a system such as ours, where we the people are Caesar, rendering unto Caesar would include all of us. In that case, it should be a religious as well as civic duty to vote.

More and more Christians began to accept that philosophy, and by the early 80's, Jerry Falwell had formed what became the Moral Majority. Many active Christians of many denominations joined that effort, and politicians became very aware of their potential impact on campaigns and careers.

Republicans especially courted the Christian votes, which tended to be more conservative. And conservative was becoming the hallmark of the Grand Old Party. Right wing evangelical leaders moved swiftly to join the efforts of Ronald Reagan. Although he was divorced and remarried, anathema to many conservative Christians, the message he carried was theirs.

The GOP had been shrinking for years, and the evangelical right gave party leaders new hope for rebuilding. They incorporated new planks into their platform over the years, including those opposing abortion and gay rights. Anyone running for any office would complete questionnaires including these issues.

Soon, dire warnings crept into media messages, with caveats that abortion would bring down America, and gays had an agenda to undermine traditional marriage. Fear would now be a central part of campaigning for almost any office or any issue.

Other segments of society latched onto this tool. The National Rifle Association began warning that our government would soon confiscate all guns, and we would all be defenseless. Any effort by any governmental body to limit access to certain weapons would meet the attack arm of the NRA.

Even with terrorist attacks at theaters, schools, shopping centers and churches, the NRA would condone no encroachment on their 2nd Amendment rights. The mentally ill and criminals shouldn't be allowed to have lethal weapons, but they would allow no laws with actual limits on access.

With every new effort to require background checks on everyone, the NRA media machine immediately responds that Americans will lose the right to go hunting and to defend their own homes. They scream that the government is our enemy, and yet we the people are the government.

Still, fear reigns. And today we have access to information on a level never available any time in history. They want to keep the fear growing.

Americans are terrified today of losing our rights to the government, of losing our concept of marriage, of losing the soul of our nation to abortion and contraception, of being attacked in public places by foreign terrorists or even in schools and churches by domestic terrorists.

In addition, we are bombarded by messages from politicians telling us Social Security and Medicare funds will run out, and older Americans will then be at risk of poverty. They can fix the problems, but they would rather use the programs as political tools to "scare" up votes.

The simplest adjustment is to lift the ceiling on earnings taxed to support the system. By taxing all income, 70% of the deficit could be eliminated. Raising the minimum wage would take care of the rest.

Of course, that brings another scare. Opponents of minimum wage (high or low) argue all the time that even the concept of minimum wage destroys or limits jobs. They rant that raising it would be such a burden on businesses, especially small ones, that they would eliminate jobs or even close down.

Never mind that every time the minimum was raised, the same warning arose. And every time it proved to be a lark. Jobs did not disappear; in fact, they increased. More money in the hands of the working poor meant more spending. More spending brought more increases in every part of our economy.

And it brought more tax revenue, including Social Security and Medicare, to our government coffers. And when the minimum went up, so did those wage levels above it. Everybody made more, including the rich.

Did prices rise? Of course they did, but wealth went up higher and faster. Today, we have lost balance, and that creates even more fear.

The wage gap has been discussed for years. The top one percent has seen enormous increases in wealth and compensation, while everyone else sees their stake in America eroding.

Those at the top seem impervious to the fact that one end of our economic ship can't sink without eventually taking the other end with it. They have watched the other 99% of us sink backward into the morass with seeming nonchalance.

The most immediate fear facing most Americans is the erosion of their financial capability. In today's America, wages seem barely to keep up with inflation. Retirement is becoming more and more an illusion that is unavailable to most of us.

Many retire only to keep on working in a lower paying job to subsidize the inadequate pension or Social Security. Add to that more medical costs that are not covered by Medicare, and many retired couples have to bankrupt or divorce to survive.

And politicians who talk about family values such as preventing abortion and gay marriage offer little solace to older married couples facing neither problem. They are trying to pay for food and medicine and keep their homes. Fear rules their lives.

The generation behind them is trying to prepare for a retirement that they see doesn't look promising. They see their parents struggling. Meanwhile, they are trying to pay off their college debts and help their children, who are moving back home in increasing numbers, because of the few job opportunities.

They are not gaining in income, due to stagnation in wages, while growing burdens attack them daily. Demands on them increase, as they fight everything from finances to depression. And all the while they hear the calls for fear from terrorists, economists and politicians.

The newscasts are full of warnings of terror in the streets, civil riots, each side of government claiming the other is leading us to perdition and groups like the NRA and superpacs warning us that we are losing our rights and our future. Fear rules their lives too.

And what do our children hear. They are not impervious to news on the media, including social media. They know about the terrorist attacks on schools and churches. They see movies or ads for movies with unheard of violence.

More than half have seen their parents break up their marriage, and that is not usually the most civil process. Their family is breaking apart; their social groups are breaking apart; many of their schools are breaking or consolidating for financial reasons; they see their government writhing in agony over the simplest issues; they see reports of terror and violence all around. Fear rules their lives too.

And who is trying to calm the storm in everyone's life? During the Great Depression, FDR's words calmed many people and gave them hope. How about the leaders of today? Where are they?

The leaders of the NRA want us to believe we are about to lose our guns, and we will be at the mercy of criminals and terrorists. They want to keep that fear growing.

Many Christian leaders want us to believe we are losing our right to worship God, that we are losing the right of traditional marriage, that we are losing our soul as a nation to abortion and gay rights. Many of them even pile on the fear of the "end times" and losing our chance at heaven. They want to keep that fear growing.

The party that is out of power in Washington, or even in the states, wants us to believe that every action taken by the ruling party is taking us down the path to destruction; that we are weak before our enemies; that our financial structure is doomed; that we will all soon be out of a job, desolate, lose everything we have; that we will lose our right to vote or we will be taxed to oblivion. They want to keep that fear growing.

Whole industries want us to believe our fate as a nation depends on their success. The banks, the oil and energy industry, the auto industry, agribusiness, every major industry would tell us if they fail, we all go down with them. So it is vital that the government help them. They want to keep that fear growing.

The bigots, especially those organized like the KKK, but also including "nice" Americans, want us to believe that immigrants, especially illegal immigrants, are stealing our jobs, our benefits, our economy and our culture. They are sneaking over the border, raping and pillaging. The bigots use social media to spread a lot of their hate, and more and more believe them. They want to keep the fear growing.

And not all of the fear-mongering is done from here. Foreign interventionists want us to be afraid. Terrorist groups provoke violence here and spread messages of hate. They want to divide Americans into camps, and they want us to be afraid of everyday activities.

They spread terror, fear. They have already won that battle. We now spend billions to check people at airports and other transportation hubs. We have new security measures in stores, government buildings and other public places. The cost has been enormous. The terrorist have won.

But some of the provocation has even come from our friends in the international community. Israel is not monolithic in its public sentiment. Some Israelis would drive wedges between Americans. In efforts to influence our government, some of them take sides on issues they feel affects them. They interfere with our process by buying ads to influence one side. Those ads are designed to bring fear to some Americans of gruesome outcomes of what they say are wrong actions on our part. They want to keep the fear growing.

Even our European allies at times spread fear of negative consequences, especially in financial areas. And what of the actions of China and Russia to disrupt our communications and financial markets? Countries all over the world try to influence us as their own needs dictate, and usually it is through spreading fear of consequences. Fear is their strongest weapon. And they want to keep the fear growing.

Immigration, financial ruin, social breakdown, religious persecution, loss of freedom; there is a never-ending stream of provocation to be afraid. Americans are bombarded with threats on a daily basis, from within and without.

And the fear-mongering is always from those who have the most to gain from stoking the fire. They all tend to gain by increasing their purse or increasing their numbers or both. It seems their gain is always from our loss. It is a balanced equation.

Where are the real leaders? America once sprouted true leaders, who could inspire the world. There were leaders in every field; people all over the country and the world looked to them to find real solutions. And they always seemed to arrive on the scene at just the right time.

In health care, there was Clara Barton in nursing, Fleming and Sabin in disease control. Hospitals like the Mayo Clinic, the Cleveland Clinic, Johns-Hopkins and St. Judes gave us hope of treatments that worked and longer and better lives.

In justice, great legal minds like Oliver Wendell Holmes, Thurgood Marshall, Felix Frankfurter, Clarence Darrow and so many more brought us more assurance that we might find equal justice under the law. We felt we might all more equally enjoy the fruits of our democracy.

Civil rights leaders like Martin Luther King Jr., W. E. B. DuBois, and even further back to Frederick Douglass and Sojourner Truth, stepped up to lead us toward true equality among us. We look back at how far we have come, and yet we know we have so far to go. But that will take leadership as well.

After two centuries of sometimes unbelievable political leadership, it seems we have such a dearth of capable political leaders available today. What happened to all the Jeffersons and Madisons? Where are the Calhouns, Websters, Lincolns, Roosevelts, Trumans, Eisenhowers and Reagans? And How about the Humphries, Dirksons, Bakers and Doles? Today, half the legislators who rise up to speak in the Congress border on illiterate.

Some of our so called leaders can barely muster command of their native language, let alone our attention. In most national elections today, people tend to vote against the candidate they deem more harmful. They are not enthused by either candidate, and the winner is often seen as the lesser of two evils.

As a people, we enter a new presidential term with trepidation for what the next four years will bring. We think of whether our choice as a nation will be bad or terrible. There seems to be no optimistic expectation at all.

We all fear what the new president will do, and what the Congress will fail to do. Partisanship is now more important than policy. Any action which might benefit the people is seen through the prism of whom it will benefit politically. The opposite party will fight it to prevent the political benefit to their adversaries.

Each side will claim loudly that any new program or policy will bring down the nation, if the other side prevails. Whether the issue at hand is good for the country has no bearing. If it is also good for the President, the opposition party will find a basis for opposition, even if it started as their initiative

And if it happened to originate from the opposition in Congress, even though it might be good for everyone, the administration and their allies in Congress will almost certainly oppose it.

It's almost as if we the people were disinterested viewers looking in the public window at the "government store". We can smell what is baking, but we don't have any hope of getting a slice.

No, there are no great leaders anymore. There are only pigs at the trough. Whether in industry, government, health care, justice, education or any other segment of our society, there are just self-centered, self-interested hogs stepping up to devour their share.

Nobody really wants to feed or care for the golden goose we call America. But there are plenty, who want to claim a share of the eggs. The rich and powerful make sure to get their share, and even more. The leaders, who would normally make sure the rest might get a share, are woefully scarce.

And so it is, that today the top one percent of our society sees rising fortunes in every sense. However, the rest of us are on a slippery slope toward mediocrity, due to fewer resources and fewer opportunities.

We wonder why there is such fear in the land. There was a movie some years ago called "Oh, God!" George Burns and John Denver played the lead parts. In one scene, Denver asked Burns, who was playing God, "Why do you allow such suffering in the world? Why don't you help us?" Burns replied, "That's why I gave you each other."

When we assess the problems facing us, we should all remember in the face of such growing problems, "That's why he gave us each other." We were supposed to look out for one another. That was the whole idea of America and our Constitution.

And our leaders were supposed to supply us the leadership to do that, to look out for each other. Our leaders now look out for themselves. They are the cause of our national fear. And that is the view from the bottom.

A FORMULA FOR INSIGHT

The square of the hypotenuse of any right triangle is equal to the sum of the squares of the other two sides.

The Pythagorean Theorem

Most of us learn certain basic rules of thought during our school years. Not that we learn what to think, but rather how to think, that is, how to deduce and organize our thoughts. As with any formula in mathematics or chemistry, we must acquire facts from various sources and assemble them in an organized manner in order to arrive at a reasonable conclusion.

Two parts hydrogen and one part oxygen properly joined will produce water. A right triangle with two legs measuring three and four inches will have a hypotenuse that measures five inches. These formulae are exact and always work. The formula for insight is a little less precise.

That is because every mind combines facts a little differently, and, therefore, may arrive at slightly different conclusions. We all think in a way we have learned as individuals, each having different family backgrounds, educational experiences and other life experiences. How a mind operates depends on these and any number of other factors. We all, however, have methods of thought, and each of us has thoughts or opinions on various topics.

Our opinions form our insight. And, although the formula for each of us will vary from all others, there are certain basic factors we all have in common, that is to say, the general formula is the same. We see, we hear, we assemble facts, new and old, and we think.

We combine with conversation, which gathers additional thoughts of others, parts of which we adopt for consideration along with our own facts and experiences. The resultant attitudes are our opinions. Our insight, therefore, is our understanding and interpretation of events and issues in light of our individual formulae.

It matters not whether we are corporate executives, doctors, teachers, mechanics, homemakers, accountants, lawyers, construction workers or bellhops. We each have opinions, and all are important.

How do we arrive at our opinions on such complex issues as education, health care reform, racism and all the political problems facing us today? Where do we get our basic information? How do we process it, and how do we use the final assessments?

There are thousands of newspapers across America, and they are all different. Newspapers in Washington, D.C. do not report the news exactly as does the San Francisco Examiner, the Chicago Tribune or the Cleveland Plain Dealer. Hence, the different views of those who live in these diverse areas from the views of those who live in the others or in other parts of the country.

Newspapers, television, internet and other media give us much of our basic information on the issues of the day. Small communities with local weekly newspapers have views differing even further with those of big cities. Those areas served by more than one major newspaper usually seem to have a better mix of information available.

Magazines are another important source of information. A country with a greater variety of magazines available for the public is hardly imaginable. So many specialty magazines and magazines appealing to small segments of our society assure us that public opinion will never be monolithic in America.

Americans read more magazines as a nation than any other, it would seem. And since the advent of internet magazines and blogs, we have infinite sources of information and opinions, and the dividing line between those two is not always clear.

Broadcast news and various talk and interview shows on the internet, radio and television have made us the most informed people ever to have existed on this planet. There are very few individuals in the United States that are not bombarded daily by the electronic media with information from all sources.

Some of this information is subliminal in nature. We learn and absorb without necessarily intending to do so. Radio and TV used as background noise (usually music) is interrupted regularly for newscasts and commercials. The internet is one of the most absorbing pastimes in this country. Our children become addicts early. Some Americans may use the web as there only source of news and information.

Besides the general sources such as magazines, blogs, newspapers, radio and television, we all receive brochures and various other types of propaganda through the mail. For many this constitutes a significant source of information. It is obvious when we consider the amount of direct mail and email marketing that goes on in the United States today.

Add to these the thoughts and opinions of our friends and acquaintances and the discussions we have with them, and it is easy to see that Americans have an enormous amount of information at their disposal. It is only reasonable, then, to grant the average American the respect due for opinions that as a whole are well founded.

They are at least as valid as those of many of our politicians, whose opinions seem derived many times from information obtained from special interests anxious to elect or re-elect officials who may respond to their special "needs". Nevertheless, those on the bottom do have opinions.

We may, in fact, be the most opinionated generation ever. Granted, many of those opinions in the age of computers is based on pseudo-facts picked up on the internet from dubious sources and perpetuated on the strength of conviction more than truth. But well founded or not, they are opinions and valid in exchange as if they were truth.

We have opinions on the problems that plague our nation. We think we know why our education system no longer works. We have ideas on improving the health care delivery system in America. We have thoughts on the weaknesses in our judicial system, and in our electoral system.

We know the economy is bad, and although we may not have absolute solutions, we have ideas on who has caused its failures. We have no tolerance for running our government forever in deficit and ever deeper into debt.

We are impatient with foreign policy that reflects more of the pragmatism of politicians hoping for re-election than of the ideals and compassion of our people, who yearn for true peace for all nations around the world. The vast majority of us despise racism and other divisions in our society, while some of our leaders seem to thrive on such divisive factors.

Yes, we on the bottom think. We converse among ourselves and discuss all manner of issues. We come to conclusions. We know they may not always be right, but we also know that often they are correct. What disturbs us most is that our leaders seem at times so incapable of arriving at any conclusions about anything.

We all know that our education system and its funding mechanisms need to be overhauled. Even our leaders say as much. But, what have they done besides lament the present condition.

We on the bottom know we need to revamp our entire health care delivery system even further. Even the politicians are saying so. But, it is a good bet that whatever changes are adopted, it will be a slow process over many years. We all know that crime is rampant in America today, and, yet, all we can get out of our leadership is a hapless "oh, woe are we!"

Tune in C-SPAN and watch our members of Congress give speech after speech (often to an empty chamber) damning the absence of laws and facilities and programs needed to combat crime, but there is no action to go with their words.

They raise their fists for the war on drugs, but there is no action to go with their words. They decry the loss of jobs and the poverty it spawns, but there is no action to go with their words. They condemn injustice in other lands, but there is no action to go with their words. They denounce the irresponsibility of deficit spending, but there is no action to go with their words.

They lament the decline of the American family as an institution and the resulting decay in the fabric of our society, but there is no action to go with their words. They seem to speak out on all issues affecting American life, and they speak so passionately, but there is no action to go with their words.

Why is there no action to go with their words? Is there something in the chemistry of leadership that alters thought patterns to eliminate the portion of the process that takes the step from identifying a problem to formulating solutions?

Yes, of course, we all know that there are sometimes many possible solutions to any given problem, and opinions will differ on which of the possible solutions is the best one or even an acceptable one.

That does not assuage the average American who feels that, if we on the bottom can come up with answers, those on the top with access to even more information ought to be able to solve problems and solve them faster than they have in the past. The necessity of compromise is no excuse.

In fact, it is all the more reason to expect quicker action. So often, there is no reason for inaction except to avoid alienation of voters.

After all, any decision is going to anger some. Most politicians don't want to anger anyone. It might cost an election.

But, if re-election is the most important issue to a leader, then that person has no place in political office. It is similar to the position of a parent trying always to win approval of the children for every action. A parent does not need the approval of the children, only the respect. Approval will come later, when the results come home (maturity).

Voters are no different. We may not know that an action was right until all the results are available. That may not be until after the next election. But a politician should, as a parent, take the right action necessary for the best interest of the voters (just as parents should do for children).

There are so many in high office today who seem to those of us on the bottom to be so consumed with thae desire to stay in office, that any concern for doing what is right must be addressed in the context of the next re-election campaign. The solutions, therefore, are not escaping our leaders. They are often the same solutions that occur to us. But solutions can cause new problems to some politicians.

Unfortunately, many of our leaders, whether they be politicians, business leaders, scientists, bureaucrats or technicians, have lost their connection with the general body of society. They have spent so much of their lives talking TO the rest of us, that they can no longer comfortably talk WITH us.

We all have the same basic formula for defining problems and developing solutions. The differences are societal. First, we amass information from many sources. Then we combine the new information with the experiences of our past. After exploring the subject at hand with others and digesting their ideas, we can come to meaningful conclusions about the parameters of the problems and their possible solutions.

For instance, I went to public schools for twelve years, a university for four and various technical training courses relative to my work.

I know what education was like years ago and how well the system seemed to work. I studied originally to be a teacher, and I was married to a teacher.

I understand many of the changes in society since my own school days and realize they must be taken into account. I read constantly about the problems in education in accounts in newspapers and magazines. I watch special presentations on television and the internet about today's schools and their problems. I hear discussions on radio about these problems and possible solutions.

I discuss them with friends and acquaintances. I hear and see information on systems in other countries. So, I feel I have a pretty good grasp of the subject. I have definite opinions on what the causes of the problems are and how they might be solved.

I think other people go through similar patterns of idea formulation. They may arrive at different conclusions, but together we might have common trends that could bring us to better solutions and ultimately better schools and a better system.

Through this same deliberative process the average American comes to conclusions on health care delivery and availability, crime control, child support enforcement, free trade agreements, society values, bigotry and all the many complex issues facing us every day. We use the process even to decide which candidates to support.

Is it too much to expect our politicians to look beyond their own narrow self-interest and use this process, or even listen to us, to solve our problems while they are still manageable? Is it unreasonable to expect labor leaders to seek the best interest of the rank and file who must rely on these leaders for a decent future?

Is it overbearing of the people to ask business leaders to temper their expectation of immediately greater profit with their loyalty to our country and our communities? Is it exaggeration to say that by and large the people of this country as a group have the solutions to our own problems?

We are not all scientists, but we understand some basic science. We are not all economists, but we can deal with basic budget concepts. We are not all educators, but we know what we want for our children and how we were ourselves educated.

We are not experts in medical care or insurance or law, but we know we want access to our health care system for everyone, and we know we can provide it, because other countries have. We are not all sociologists, but we are well aware of the breakdown of the American family, and we know there must be ways to fix parts of it and ultimately most of it.

And we know we are diverse and divided as a people. That is both good and bad. We know there are ways to amplify the good, while diminishing the bad. We are not all experts in criminology, but we know crime is a plague in our society and must be stopped, not just discussed.

Moreover, we are not all politicians, but we are all political. We know our system has been and continues to be abused, and we know it can work better for all of us. We have opinions in all these areas and countless others.

Our opinions are formed in the same way as those of the experts at the top. Though they may not be as precise or technically founded, they are, nevertheless, important considerations in the America we know today.

In a nation that is governed by its own people, their will and, therefore, their opinion must be paramount. If there are sound reasons for straying from the will of the people, they should be explained in light of the facts that were unavailable to the rest of us. We will understand.

We have that capacity. But, overall, we feel we have a right to expect our leaders to measure up to the trust we have given them, and we expect our views to be considered. We believe our views to be valid factors for consideration by those at the top, along with any other information they are processing. As they accommodate each other's views, those at the top should always try to see also the view from the bottom.